Shelena, Kevin, Gary

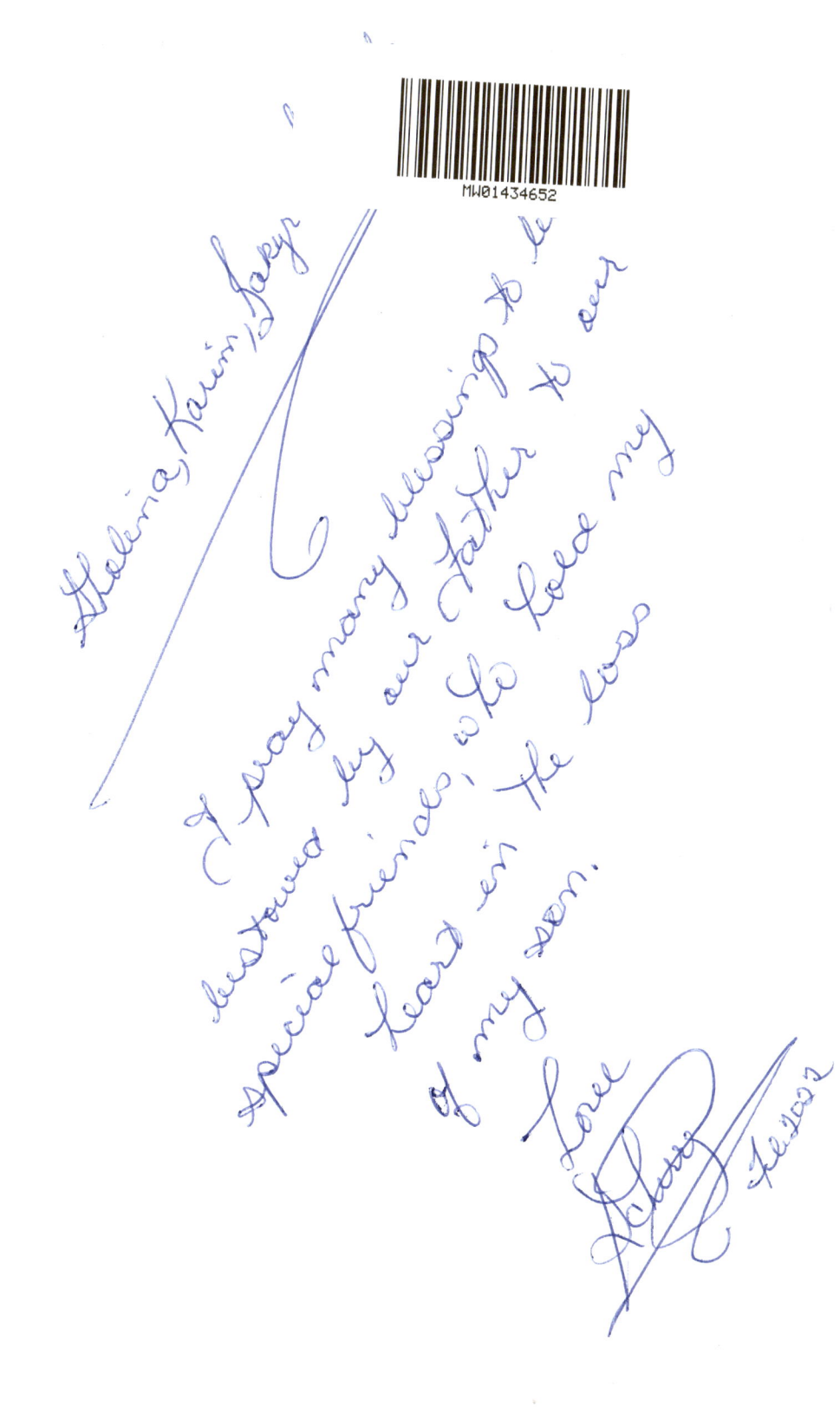

I pray many blessings to be bestowed by our father to our special friends, who to hold my heart in the loss of my son.

Love
[signature]

BUT GOD, I DON'T WANT TO WRITE A BOOK!

Scherry George

WestBow
PRESS
A DIVISION OF THOMAS NELSON
& ZONDERVAN

Copyright © 2021 Scherry George.

All rights reserved. No part of this book may be used or reproduced by any means, graphic, electronic, or mechanical, including photocopying, recording, taping or by any information storage retrieval system without the written permission of the author except in the case of brief quotations embodied in critical articles and reviews.

This book is a work of non-fiction. Unless otherwise noted, the author and the publisher make no explicit guarantees as to the accuracy of the information contained in this book and in some cases, names of people and places have been altered to protect their privacy.

WestBow Press books may be ordered through booksellers or by contacting:

WestBow Press
A Division of Thomas Nelson & Zondervan
1663 Liberty Drive
Bloomington, IN 47403
www.westbowpress.com
844-714-3454

Because of the dynamic nature of the Internet, any web addresses or links contained in this book may have changed since publication and may no longer be valid. The views expressed in this work are solely those of the author and do not necessarily reflect the views of the publisher, and the publisher hereby disclaims any responsibility for them.

Any people depicted in stock imagery provided by Getty Images are models, and such images are being used for illustrative purposes only. Certain stock imagery © Getty Images.

Scripture taken from the New King James Version®. Copyright © 1982 by Thomas Nelson. Used by permission. All rights reserved.

ISBN: 978-1-6642-4695-9 (sc)
ISBN: 978-1-6642-4820-5 (hc)
ISBN: 978-1-6642-4696-6 (e)

Library of Congress Control Number: 2021920701

Print information available on the last page.

WestBow Press rev. date: 01/07/2022

CONTENTS

Foreword ix
Introduction xi

Chapter 1 1
    I Wanted to Sing!
    My Spiritual Journey Begins
    First Confirmation of Task
    Second Confirmation of Task
    Divine Direction
    God's Message of Encouragement
    Tithes
    Book of Remembrance

Chapter 2 15
    Come Into Being
    Love, Faith and Believe
    Baby Discernment
    Early Childhood
    The Seed First Planted

Chapter 3 27
    Pain Transference
    Prayerful Intersession
    Heaven's Fragrance

Gift of Tongues
  Disillusioned
  Stranded and Lost, But Not Alone
  The Good Samaritans
  Dancing with the Devil

Chapter 4 45
  A Destiny Fulfilled
  Ghostly Visitor
  Lifted by Angels
  Lucid Dreams
  God Was Calling Me
  Divine Intervention
  A Celebration
  Deliverance from Danger
  Take Off Your Shoes

Chapter 5 73
  Michael's Premonition
  My Beloved Michael Murdered
  Grand Foyer Revisited
  Wall of Angels
  Saying Goodbye
  I Love You Mama
  Baby Consoler
  Michael Visits Sarah
  Michael Listened In
  Comforter or Comforted
  Michael Visits His Dad
  Lenny

Chapter 6 99
  God's Grace and Mercy
  Jenny's Healing

I'm Alright
Baptized
Forgiveness of a Lie
"Mommy, I've Been Murdered"
Count Your Blessings
Understanding God's Sacrifice

Chapter 7 115
Blessed Assurance
I Saw What You Did
God Encircles His Children
Forerunner Vision
Ghostly Visitor Returns
God First, Then You
The Reluctant Gift
God's Reward
Phyllis's Cross
But God, I Don't Want to Write a Book!
Cross Finale
Jenny Saved

Chapter 8 139
God Manifested Good
Toonie on the Floor
The Spirit Spoke
Spiritual Impartation
Grace Sergeant
He That is Within Me
How Great Thou Art
God's Perfect Timing
Flowers Flourished
Welcome Home
Michael's Last Visit

Chapter 9 167
    God's Favour
    God Restored My Heart
    Last But Not Least

Acknowledgements... 185
Epilogue.. 189
    Sinner's Prayer

FOREWORD

But God, I Don't Want To Write A Book! is written by my dear friend Scherry George, whom I have had the pleasure of knowing for over 18 years. I have also had the privilege of working with her as well, and have witnessed or heard of these encounters. This book is a captivating, thought-provoking, awe-inspiring account of her life experiences and divine encounters. Scherry was inspired by God to diarize these extraordinary events of her life, not knowing that God had intended on her to write this book. **For I know the thoughts that I think toward you, says the Lord, thoughts of peace and not of evil, to give you future and a hope. - Jeremiah 29:11**

The mere and simple act of picking up this book signifies that you are intrigued and ready to indulge in the splendidly textured events that occurred in her life that will have you desiring more. The title of this book will identify with everyone who has ever struggled with self-doubt, fearing the unknown, aiming to decipher their purpose, or trying to grasp the "why's" of life. Love, grief, forgiveness, hope, faith, loss, servanthood, marriage, navigating relationships through crises, spiritual and supernatural encounters; are just a few examples of what you will uncover as you read through these pages, and be enamoured by her shared experiences.

The encounters depicted in this book will challenge, inspire, and have you taking an introspective look on your own life. One quickly recognizes, as you delve further into the book, it will shed light on your very own uncommon encounters and experiences. It also speaks to the desire of living out our purpose in life as God intended, illuminating the constant struggle we often experience in being obedient to the voice of God or the call to serve Him and mankind. May it be feeding the homeless, being in the right place at the right time, valuing the moments you have with your loved ones and, or always, being obedient to voice of God, doing as He prompts. As the scripture states, **But he who is greatest among you shall be your servant. - Matthew 23:11.**

Scherry strongly believes that there are no coincidences in Christ and that everything we are privileged to experience in this life is as God intended and I could not agree more. This book is filled with many insights that will have you asking pivotal questions that will question your thinking, and in most cases, defy societal norms, culture, education, religion and even our own personal beliefs and upbringing. It will encourage and empower you to not be afraid to go off the beaten path, to be different, follow your heart, incline your ears to hear the voice of God. **Incline your ear and come to Me. Hear and your soul shall live; - Isaiah 55:3a**

There are so many ways this book has impacted my life, it may be the divine encounters and beautiful experiences that so many of us dream of experiencing, at least once in our lifetime. I passionately believe in sharing our stories because we never know the life-changing impact it may have on another individual. I am also reminded me that we are never alone, that the Lord watches over us and that He is in the business of communicating with His people. I am excited for the effect this book will have on the lives of its readers. My hope is that, as you read this book, you will become empowered to empower others, strive to not only to answer His call but to listen, and be obedient. Everyone has a story to tell, may you be encouraged and empowered to tell yours.

Georgiana Collington

INTRODUCTION

And he who has seen has testified, and his testimony is true; and he knows that he is telling the truth, so that you may believe. - John 19:35

Writing this book is my fulfilment of an act of obedience to God and a celebration of His majesty in my life. Written herein, is a compilation of my truths regarding the wonderous experiences I have witnessed, since before my birth, to the present time.

Why me? I do not know and it is not for me to wonder why. It is simply because God ordains it to be so! He has given me many wonderful and marvelous things in my life to share. He has given me a spirit of obedience; although my human nature wanted to ignore writing a book all these many years, I can no longer ignore the task. And because He is persistent! You will find in these pages many instances when I was being obedient and receptive to the urging of the Holy Spirit, how situations worked in miraculous fashion and how I and others were ultimately blessed in the outcomes.

It is important to acknowledge that through all these blessings, I have been as amazed and as surprised as you may be, reading about them within these pages. I often wondered if I was imagining God's active participation in my life, but then He finds a way to confirm His intention and my actions, so I continue to listen to the prompting He provides to do the things He asks of me. I do not profess to be more holy or a more religious person. I do not profess in any way or manner to be more important than anyone else, I do not profess that I am loved more than anyone else - far from it. I am an ordinary person, chock-full of flaws and failings, weaknesses, imperfections and short-comings. I do, however, declare that He has given me a spirit attuned to His promptings and I learned to listen to His spiritual whispers and let Him guide my actions and light my path. I have also learned if I don't listen to the promptings the first time, God will be persistent in getting my attention! I may have, in my imperfect nature, missed some things but the things I am sharing are the things I have lived, witnessed and can truthfully testify to.

In His infinite wisdom God touched me throughout the years with experiences that sometimes seemed fantastical. Although I appreciated that there was something special about His favour to bless me in this regard, I did not for a very long time connect the dots that I should write a book specifically about my experiences. I wish I had recognized my intended task earlier to have recorded actual dates and time and more detail. But I believe God has directed my path and led me to write the things I would have otherwise forgotten.

What has been remembered foremost in this account, are the many instances and events that unfolded. I have recorded specific detail of the dates and of the time where I did recall or made notes. Later in life I started to take this book writing task more seriously because I could no longer ignore what was unfolding in my life, and I started to sporadically document what I was experiencing.

Where discerned throughout writing this book, I have provided scripture from the New King James Version (NKJV) that speaks to my personal interpretation of my experiences and I rely on the Holy Spirit to guide me and lead me on this journey. Therefore, not surprisingly, scripture crystalized clearly to me my task ahead during my daily devotions throughout November and December 2020; to begin writing this book and to support my written testimony.

May God bless you, as He has blessed me.

CHAPTER 1

I Wanted to Sing!

**May He grant you according to your heart's *desire*,
And fulfill all your purpose. - Psalm 20:4**

I have always wanted to sing like my mother, Verdena Frances Borden. My mother had one of those God given natural voices with a resonance that made the hair stand up on the back of my neck because her sound was so rich and harmonious. Dare I say, her voice was heavenly! My much loved, and dearly missed mother passed away August 28, 2020, at the age of ninety-four in her sleep, may she rest in peace. God was gracious in her passing.

As a little girl, I wanted to be like her, look like her and especially sound just like her. Alas, it was not to be, the singing at least! At best, I had the singing voice of a frog growing up. Not only could I not sing, but for some reason I could barely speak into early evening. My voice left me early in the evening hours, and the best I could muster was a very frustrating squeaking sound whenever I attempted to say something. The next morning my voice would return to normal until the next evening.

But from an early age, I could write. God gives everyone a gift, and mine was writing. I also had an inordinate number of unusual experiences and my mom used to say to me, "Child you should write a book." I won a six-grade school writing contest in 1965 and it was supposed to be a big event. Prince Philip was supposed to come to our school, King Edward Elementary School, in Saint John New Brunswick, to present the Duke of Edinburgh Awards as well as make presentations to the students who had won the different levels of the writing contest.

I was so excited and looking forward to it. Not only had I earned the Bronze Level Duke of Edinburgh Award for physical fitness, for my proficiency on the trampoline, I had also won the Grade Six Writing Prize for my essay on Albert Schweitzer. At the last minute there was some change in Prince Philip's schedule; he didn't come and they sent someone else. I was deeply disappointed, so much so that I didn't cherish my writing prize, which was a hard cover red book. I kept it as a keepsake for many years but over the course of growing up, I misplaced it. I'm not sure what ultimately happened to the book or even what it was about. I still, however, have and cherish my Duke of Edinburgh Bronze Level Certificate.

Although I enjoyed writing throughout my life and wrote poems and essays that I treasured, I didn't want to write a book – writing a book seemed like such a huge chore, *I wanted to sing*!

My Spiritual Journey Begins

Behold, I stand at the door and knock. If anyone hears My voice and opens the door, I will come in to him and dine with him, and he with Me. - Revelation 3:20

Like many of you reading this book, I am saved, blessed and a highly favoured child of God, having had a personal relationship with Jesus since I was about seven or eight. I remember the Easter service my mom and dad took my younger siblings, Lynn and Kevin, and I to church. This was a special occurrence. I don't recall ever going to church with my mom and dad, although they made sure us children went regularly.

I guess because it was Easter, we went to a "big" church, not our neighbourhood church for the special service. I recall the Calvary Temple Church was big and ornately extravagant in my young experience. I don't recall much of the service until the end when there was an altar call for anyone who wanted to accept Jesus in his or her life. I had never been to a service that had an altar call or even knew what an altar call was. This was my first introduction to the concept of accepting Jesus in my life, although I did not consciously understand what was happening.

When the altar call came, we had been kneeling. I was anxious and my heart was rapidly beating because I felt I just *had to* go to answer the call. I stood up. As I started to leave the pew, my dad reached over to me and lightly touched me on the arm and gently whispered for me to sit down. There was no malice intended, and as I think back, I believe dad may have felt I didn't know what I was committing to. At the time I was so glad he had stopped me because I was so fearful in that very moment. I sat down, relieved that I didn't have to go to the front of the church. I believe in my heart, however, that although I sat down, Jesus saw my heart and saved me in that very instant that I stood up.

Before this moment, I had already experienced unusual situations and supernatural occurrences, although I was too young at the time to articulate them in that manner, but I did know there were things happening beyond my understanding. Since that first day I stood up to accept Jesus, to now, I have been in and out of organized church but God has never let go of me, has never forsaken me, and has kept His hand of mercy and grace upon my life as you will see as I continue to share my spiritual journey with you.

First Confirmation of Task

In Him also we have obtained an inheritance, being predestined according to the purpose of Him who

works all things according to the counsel of His will, that we who first trusted in Christ should be to the praise of His glory. - Ephesians 1:11-12

Unexpectedly, one summer day approximately around 2006, I got a surprise workplace visit from my former colleague Georgiana, one of the sweetest, God-fearing women I have ever had the pleasure to know. She had changed jobs and moved away years before but she reached out unexpectedly and came to see me, specifically to tell me that God told her to tell me that *I needed to write a book.*

I laughed out loud, not at Georgiana, not at the message but at the fact that, over the years I had been ignoring the promptings to write a book because I didn't want to do it. I admitted to Georgiana that she was, in fact, confirming what God had been speaking to me over the years. In good humour, I told her I would "take it under further consideration," and left it at that. I knew Georgiana was being obedient to God by visiting me after such a long absence to give me His message. I knew God was speaking to me through her and knew I had to write a book someday, whether I wanted to or not, but again put it in the back of my mind.

Many more years passed and I continued to procrastinate, thinking I would write the book *someday*. With the idea always in the back of my mind, I found any number of excuses not to do it. I was bringing up my children, working a highly successful career, didn't have the time, and so on and so on. God continued to shower me with the many events I am sharing with you in this book and continued to show me His awesome power even though I was yet not obedient to His prompting.

My someday is today - December 1, 2020.

I offer my sincerest thanks to Georgiana for her obedience in sharing God's message for me, with me, back in 2006. Over a long period of time, after Georgiana's visit, I came to understand I did have to write a book, but not just any book - specifically *this book* to share with you, all that the Lord has been to me, shown to me and blessed me. I am simply an instrument in His plan for my life and this book is the next chapter of His plan for me.

Georgiana kindly penned the Foreword to this book. God set her on this path with me, beginning with her unexpected visit in 2006.

Second Confirmation of Task

Then the Lord answered me and said: "Write the vision And make *it* plain on tablets, That he may run who reads it. For the vision *is* yet for an appointed time; But at the end it will speak, and it will not lie. - Habakkuk 2:2-3

In November 2020, when I was being led by my daily scripture reading, God confirmed to me my task was at hand through the Habakkuk scripture noted above. My spirit was compelled by this revelation, as confirmation, that I indeed had to write this book and write it *now*. No more excuses, no more delays. The Lord had given me a favoured path throughout my life with my profession, my opportunities and my success. I was now free of all the delaying tactics, rationales and self-explanations I had previously held in front of me to postpone and procrastinate getting on with my task. The time had come, and I had to give in to my calling.

I found it surreal and a bit scary that the Lord was speaking to me so clearly in His word. Scriptures I had read many times before, not only in my personal daily devotions, but in my long and checkered church life, that previously had not in any way resonated with me. I did not previously hear His word and direction for me as distinctly was being presented to me now.

The realization that God was speaking to me through His word was fearsome and frightening in the context that I could no longer ignore the prompting of the Spirit, and that I had to actually begin this journey. I still did not want to write a book but at this point

I understood I had no choice, I turned it over to Him. I prayed and continue to pray for knowledge, understanding, discernment, wisdom, direction, design, memory, mercy, compassion, honesty, truthfulness, integrity, loyalty, obedience, courage, inspiration and love. I continue to also pray for any other quality He deems necessary for me to complete this task.

I understand all things in my life have led to this, God's ultimate plan for my life. I therefore give myself as His devoted instrument.

To God be the glory and deserving of all praise.

Divine Direction

"When my soul fainted within me, I remembered the Lord; And my prayer went *up* to You, Into Your holy temple.

But I will sacrifice to You With the voice of thanksgiving; I will pay what I have vowed Salvation is of the Lord." - Jonah 2:7, 9

I initially started to write beginning in 2012 and after writing the first few pages, I contacted Georgiana and told her, "I started writing the book." That early start was eight years ago and then I put it away again. But now at the tail end of 2020, I am committed. Why now? Again, because true to form, He won't let me go! Through a dream, related or not, I was given a specific deadline to complete a major project by June 3, and it is now December. I was not at first sure the project in my dream was related to this book, but having recently retired, being fully ensconced in the worldwide changes of COVID-19, and with nowhere to go, and nothing to do, what project could I otherwise have? It is futile for me to continue to ignore His prompting to put pen to paper. God has clearly led me through my daily devotion to understand it is time to do this now, as I am otherwise free and can no longer find or justify a reason not to. The time has come - no more delays!

Like any Christian, I read my Bible. Actually, I am on my third reading through of the Bible and as magnificent as the Bible is, I've often felt it didn't speak directly to me, in my life and my day-to-day existence, that was until a few weeks ago. My many life experiences have led me to believe *there are no coincidences in Christ*; even leading me through His word to start my writing journey!

"There are no coincidences in Christ," is far more than a refrain, rather a strong belief I hold, and will be illustrated to you as I share my lived experiences contained throughout these pages.

My daily morning devotions consist of worship, prayer, Bible reading of two or three chapters as I am led, and ending with more prayer and worship. On this third reading through the Bible, nearing the end of the Old Testament, I was reading Jonah and His message jumped out at me, the passages resonated personally in my spirit. God was speaking directly to me! I discerned the Lord was telling me He wanted me to write this book *now*! The chapters of the Old Testament from Jonah through to Malachi in my daily readings gave me pause to hear His voice, directing me to where He wants me to go in taking up this task. I listened to the prompting of the Holy Spirit and although the complete chapters spoke to me, I found direction in specific verses that started me on this writing journey.

Through Jonah's experience, I understood the many mercies provided to me from God and how He has held onto me. I have known for many years I should write this book and I needed to cease ignoring God's task for me and celebrate all He has provided by sharing my story of His mercy and grace. I was also convicted that He would bring me to a place of obedience unless I stopped and listened to this calling.

Here is the conversation that God had with me through His word, all taken from NKJV over a period of some weeks:

- ❖ **"Arise, go to Nineveh, that great city, and preach to it the message that I tell you." So Jonah arose and went to Nineveh, according to the word of the Lord. - Jonah 3:2-3** I understood now was time to write this book and it was futile to try to run any longer from God's presence. This was a heart-stopping revelation for me that the messages were coming through these scriptures and were speaking directly to me, leading me down this path. Over days of devotion, the messages continued to flow and became crystal clear, I had to do what I was being led to do.
- ❖ **"But truly I am full of power by the Spirit of the Lord, And of justice and might. He has shown you, O man, what *is* good; And what does the Lord require of you But to do justly, To love mercy, And to walk humbly with your God?" - Micah 3:8 and 6:8** Scripture encouraged me I am able and could write this book because God is leading me and has shown me many good things. His task for me is to record the many blessings accurately and honestly and give Him all the glory for all that He has done in my life.
- ❖ **"The book of the vision of Nahum the Elkoshite." - Nahum 1:1** As my reading progressed, and I read Nahum was given a vision, I understood God speaks to us in many ways. This scripture resonated with me through a dream outlining the deadline to complete a major project, placing a sense of urgency in my spirit to get this underway now. I had to recognize this book as that major project.
- ❖ **"But the Lord is in His holy temple. Let all the earth keep silence before Him." - Habakkuk 2:20** I was spiritually chastised while in prayer, to listen for His voice and gently chided by the Holy Spirit to, *Be quiet*. Sometimes in prayer I spend too much time talking, instead of listening. I was still questioning whether God was really speaking to me and directing me to write this book. His word was directing me to listen to His voice and not my own.

- ❖ **"My Spirit remains among you; do not fear!" - Haggai 2:5** Through His word, God continued to tell me He is with me and not to be afraid to write this book. This scripture encouraged me to have faith and trust in the Holy Spirit for direction, submit myself to God in this task completely, and believe this is what He wants me to do.
- ❖ **"And the Lord said to Satan, 'The Lord rebuke you, Satan!' The Lord who has chosen Jerusalem rebuke you! *Is* this not a brand plucked from the fire?" - Zechariah 3:2** God showed me the enemy will try to step in with lies and discouragement and try to instill self-doubt to turn me from this book but the Lord has rebuked him from my task and I say, "Thank You Lord."
- ❖ **"Not by might, nor by power, but by My Spirit" - Zechariah 4:6** This reflected God's encouragement to me. Not in my doing but by His power, His knowledge, His strength, His wisdom and most of all by His grace I will complete this task He has set before me. Although I refer to my writing this book as a task, I realize I am chosen to do this work and am therefore blessed.

Many years ago, when I was about seventeen, I was having a cup of tea and when I had finished drinking, I discovered the teabag had broken and there at the bottom of the cup, the leaves formed a perfect lampstand. Surprised, I had never experienced seeing anything like that before. Although I did think it strange at the time to see something so clearly formed in my cup, I didn't give much thought to that lampstand in all these years until reading Zechariah. Scripture tells that God provided a vision of a lampstand to His chosen people. In my case, for such a time as this, confirming that I am on His chosen path.

Through the above scriptures I spiritually discerned that this book became His book and was destined to come to fruition through my act of love and obedience to the Father. I started writing on

December 1, 2020 when I had finished reading Zechariah but the Lord continued to quicken my spirit to the end of the Old Testament.

When I discover personal enlightenment and discernment, which corresponds to what I am writing, where fitting or appropriate, I will share scripture with you.

God's Message of Encouragement

Why are you cast down, O my soul? And why are you disquieted within me? Hope in God; For I shall yet praise Him, The help of my countenance and my God. - Psalm 43:5

Just as I had finished my first draft writing of the Introduction, I reached out by text to Georgiana on December 14, 2020. Although I have not had any contact with her since 2012, eight years ago, I wrote to tell her I seriously started, again, to write the book and to ask if she would read the introduction and confirm what I had written. Not even sure the number I had for her was her current number. Georgiana had moved away many years prior to her unexpected workplace visit in 2006 and since 2012 when I contacted her, I hadn't spoken to her. I sent her a text anyway and she responded the same day with a voice message with a revelation from God that I have saved, for encouragement. This is not the first time that Georgiana has been a conduit for the Lord in my life. I have always trusted her spiritual impartations implicitly.

To further illustrate there are no coincidences in Christ, here is what transpired when she responded by voice message. On December 14, 2020, Georgiana told me she had a dream about me *just the previous night* - keep in mind, we have had no contact whatsoever in 8 years, since 2012! The nature of her dream was disquieting as I appeared despondent, leading Georgiana to pray for me. During her prayers for me her spirit led her to recall Psalm 43:5, as quoted above.

Although she said her dream was disquieting, through her

reading of the Psalm and subsequent prayer, the Lord laid a message on her heart for me. Here is the hopeful message which she shared via voice text: "He is with you, put your hope and trust in Him. Hope in things you cannot see, knowledge in the things that God has done for you and remind you that He has brought you through the fire and He is with you always and you are not alone and to be encouraged. He tells you that the things He has done for you thus far will not compare to the things He has in store. He loves you and cherishes you. He tells you that there is more in store for you in your latter days than in your early days and it will change the trajectory of your life and the lives of others." Georgiana expressed in the voice email that she was surprised to hear from me to which I responded, "I am not at all surprised that God gave you that dream last night. As I wrote to you this morning, *there are no coincidences in Christ.*"

What an awesome God we serve!

Tithes

"Bring all the tithes into the storehouse, That there may be food in My house, And try Me now in this," Says the Lord of hosts, "If I will not open for you the windows of heaven And pour out for you *such* blessing That *there will* not *be room* enough *to receive it.*" - Malachi 3:10

Throughout my daily devotional Bible reading to complete the Old Testament and after reading about tithes and what the Lord had laid in store for me to do, I humbly submit the contents of this book as representation of my tithes for the glorious impartation of the Holy Spirit in my life.

This scripture confirms He has blessings in store for my life, as prophesied by Georgiana as she prayed. More surprisingly, she confirmed a prophetic word from God, shared with me by my older sister Karen, when I retired last September in 2020. His message to her to share with me was, "You have much yet to accomplish and He has great things in store for your life, more so than He has given you to this point in life." These separate prophesies are not a coincidence, they are spiritual confirmation of His intended plans for my life.

The significance of the message that God has more in store for my life at this late stage of my life is significant, particularly because I have had an illustrious career with 40 years of accomplishments, kudos, awards and recognition. I recently retired well-known, regarded and respected in my profession because God has shone His light on me throughout my career. I worked hard, but recognize the supernatural favour in the hearts and minds with those to whom I came into contact. I share this not as a source of immodesty, but to signify that He has done great things in my life thus far, throughout my long career, and I can only imagine what else He could have in store at this late stage of my life.

I thank God for His hand on my life and could not have asked for any higher personal or professional achievements. The thought that God has more in store for my life is too overwhelming to comprehend.

Book of Remembrance

So a book of remembrance was written before Him. For those who fear the Lord And meditate on His name. - Malachi 3:16

I continued on with my daily devotions to find this confirmation repeated to me, yet again, in Malachi that this book must be written to record and to remember all the marvels and wonders He has shown me and to share them with you. This message, as a "book of remembrance," not just a book, was first spiritually given to me in April 2008, after suffering a devastating family loss in 2007.

Early one Sunday morning in April 2008, when I was preparing to go to church, I was singing a chorus hymn "Bless the Lord, oh my soul and all that is with in me." My spirit awakened me to a recent dream I had in which a church elder told me that "God is looking out for you". As I continued preparing for church I silently wondered, *Why I am favoured as such and possess so many wonderful experiences in my life when I am not as religious as so many others in the church, yet He continues to bless me?"*. The response was swift in my spirit: *So you will write them down!* God in His infinite mercy was relentless in presenting His task for me.

God was preparing me to write this book by first planting the seed at an early age and having Georgiana speak to me and confirm His desire in 2006. Persistent, God speaking to my spirit to write a book of remembrance, in 2008. Finally, my reading of the Jonah, through Malachi scriptures, in November 2020, was scriptural confirmation that His time had come for me to get on with His task for me to write this book. I continue to declare *there are no coincidences in Christ.*

I strongly reiterate that I cannot explain any of the circumstances as I write this book. All I can do is report what I recall honestly to the best of my ability and pray the Lord, using me as His instrument, will light my path and guide my words for His purpose.

CHAPTER 2

Come Into Being

At that time Jesus answered and said, "I thank You, Father, Lord of heaven and earth, that You have hidden these things from *the* wise and prudent and have revealed then to babes." - Matthew 11:25

I was standing waiting to be born. Two other people stood with me and a tall, slim, male figure dressed in white was giving us instructions for our next step in our respective spiritual journeys. I have no recollection of anything prior to this event except understanding that we had each personally made it to reach this point and our next step was to come to this earth. This earth journey was meant to be a period of growth, a test for myself, as well as the two other people.

We possessed knowledge of the universe and we had completed our steps to bring us to this point in our spiritual growth. I use the term *people* in this context because we had, in essence, "graduated" into our physical bodies for this next stage of our growth. As part of our preparation, death was explained to us and we were told that our life on earth would end and we would return to this place. There was no experience of death in this place where we were to compare to, so I really did not comprehend the fullness of the concept of death in my pending journey. I cannot speak to the experience of the other people alongside me, I can only speak to my experience.

My experience while standing there led me to believe we clearly understood that the earthly life on which we were embarking was a spiritual test. Our role was to physically come to earth, to love, believe and have faith that a Higher Power exists, and possess the knowledge we would be returned to this place after death for the next phase of our development.

How we loved, had faith in the greater Power and believed we would return to this place after our deaths to continue our journey, were the ultimate determinants over everything else of the lives we were going to lead and what "level" we would progress to, once we returned.

We were gathered in front of a large globe which was positioned sitting inside a high pedestal. Looking deep into the globe, we were able to see the earth. It was here we were able to choose where and to whom we wanted to be born to begin this journey. It was then I chose my parents. We were filled with knowledge of the earth to make our decisions. I distinctly remember that I chose my parents specifically because they were Black and poor, and I believed that these were challenges that I could easily meet once born. How little I understood the true test to come.

Standing there I arrogantly felt I could come here under earthly adverse conditions, persevere and pass this physical "life" test. I am vaguely aware that as we talked together, I was also told that part of my spiritual journey would be that I would lose a significant person in my life to this "death" and that part of my challenge for growth would be how I worked through that. Such arrogance - not having a concept of death at the time, I remember thinking, *This will be a breeze!* I knew so little at that time about what this life would truly entail and what it would ultimately mean for me.

Since being born, many thoughts and memories have arisen in my consciousness. Of course, many more probably have not and I cannot speak to the memories that have since been lost to my subconscious unless or until they are brought forward by the grace and loving-kindness of the Holy Spirit.

Love, Faith and Believe

And now abide faith, hope, love, these three; but the greatest of these *is* love. - 1 Corinthians 13:13

I have no recollection of being born Scherry Demarge Shepherd in Saint John, New Brunswick, Canada, on May 4, 1953 but I do remember laying in my crib as a baby. The first thing I remember is that I felt extremely heavy. The lightness I felt before I came was gone. While standing at the pedestal, I was light and free. Now here I was trapped in a heavy body over which I had no physical control. My mind was clear but I could not communicate. Not only was my mind clear, I was struck with a growing uneasiness and fear because I soon realized my memory was fading more and more. Every day I remembered less than the day before. I came to the conscious realization that by the time I learned to talk, I would have forgotten all *"the knowledge"* that I had before I was born!

I began to realize this was going to be the real test - to love, believe and have faith in a Higher Power and know there was life after death – without the benefit of the prior knowledge! Before, when standing at the pedestal, I hadn't realized I would lose all the knowledge once I was born. Once I understood that I would have to do this test without the knowledge that I had been sent off with and been born with, I *now* understood the magnitude of the test. I realized this was not going to be a breeze. I was scared and felt trapped in my infant body.

My mind raced and I thought to try to remember at least one bit of knowledge or truth to hold on to before they all slipped away, forgotten. The one memory I kept repeating was, "I chose my parents." This is the only knowledge I came away with and can share with you.

Life progressed. My memories of the knowledge were erased except what I have written above. Growing up, in my heart I always knew I had chosen my parents but it was not something I often or openly spoke about or thought about until later in life. On those rare occasions when I would share some of the marvels that God has given to me with trusted friends and family, people often would comment, "You should write a book." They were amazed at the experiences I shared. Strangely enough, although I had these experiences, day-to-day living put these things in the background of my mind until I brought them forth, for such a time as writing this book.

Baby Discernment

"Take heed that you do not despise one of these little ones, for I say to you that in heaven their angels always see the face of My Father who is in heaven." - Matthew 18:10

I have always marveled at babies, wondering if they shared the experiences I had, if they had any recollection of before they were born like I had. Wondering did they still have the knowledge as I held them and cuddled them? What would they say if they could talk to me? When I see their eyes following invisible movements around the room, I wonder, what are they seeing, what experiences are they having? I didn't see flying angels as a child but later in life I came to have personal knowledge of their divine presence. I have firsthand knowledge - not remembered but lived – that they, angels are here with us to watch over and protect and guide us. I am confident we each are born with our own spiritual gifts, our own experiences, and I hope mine will give you pause to think of your own life and journey.

Later on, I will share a poignant example of discernment expressed by a baby, experienced while many witnesses looked on in shocked amazement.

There are so many things we do not know and cannot explain but are real in our respective lives. When my third child, Sarah, was very young about four years old, she could see people's auras. She would often say, "Mommy look at that lady or man and all the pretty colour around her or him." She would tell me whatever colour she was seeing surrounding the person at that given moment.

I didn't comprehend at first what she was seeing and describing, but it eventually dawned on me she had to be seeing people's energy through their auras. What else could it be that she was seeing? This phenomenon went on for many years -so much so it had become common place with her. I didn't think much about her being able to actually see people's energy in that way; it was just something Sarah was naturally able to do. Over time she stopped commenting on seeing the colours and I simply thought Sarah had grown out of this ability.

At the time she was experiencing these things as a child, I didn't think about documenting it until I started thinking and writing about all the strange occurrences in my life. When I gave Sarah this portion of the book to read to ensure I had written it correctly she informed me that her ability to see auras, did not exactly end in childhood. She has tried to explain to me that her vision has always, even now, incorporated colours much like pixels or tv static. I have a hard time comprehending her experience.

More recently, in her early adult life, when she met her husband Jonathon for the very first time in 2008, she was able to see his aura. Sarah tells me she was sitting in the Centennial College Student Centre and she saw him come in. He was walking towards her table where she was sitting with a friend. Jonathon had an outline of a gold aura. Sarah thought this was unique. Although she had seen auras before, this was the first time she witnessed a gold aura so she knew in her heart he was special. The friend she was sitting with introduced them and Sarah noted that she thought he was nice, as well as handsome. It was a short first meeting and they encountered each other on two more occasions, but Jon did not remember her. The third time they met they discovered how much they had in common. Almost two weeks passed and they decided to become exclusive.

Sarah and Jon had quietly established their relationship with one another. During this time, she had not shared with me and her dad that she had met him. So, when she came to me out of the blue one day and said, "Mom I met someone," I could have fallen over. This statement was coming from a young lady who had never before indicated any interest in any young man and quite frankly I was stunned. It was the last thing I would have imagined was going to come out of her mouth.

The timing was delicate, it was a relatively short period after we suffered a family tragedy which I will later share. Due to this tragedy, I was overly protective of my daughter. When she said she had met someone, my entire being went into so many emotions in what seemed like two seconds: disbelief, fear, anxiety, terror, and curiosity. Who was this person, where did he come from? Sarah must have known I was about to go into shock so before I could utter one word, she looked at me, dead-panned and stoically like only she can, and said the words that instantaneously calmed me and made everything all right!

Sarah said, "Mom he is saved. His name is Jonathon Mitchell." Actually, I didn't hear his name right away, all I heard was he was saved. The words every Christian mother longs to hear – "he's saved!" Sarah walked her own walk and it wasn't until she found "the one" that she came and acknowledged to her father and I that there was a man, a God-fearing man, in her life.

Only God! Only God when I wasn't watching or wasn't seeing due to my own internal struggles at the time, God was looking after Sarah. Not only was He looking after her but He gave her the best He had, His born-again child Jonathon. God has a way of putting people in our lives and in our paths to glorify Himself and to give us encouragement and strength in our walk with Him. I believe God presented Jonathon to Sarah when she needed him most in her life and in His wisdom presented Jonathon with the sweetest, nicest, young lady he'd obviously ever met, or would meet. My daughter is, and remains a treasure, now to Jon as well as to her sister Chantal, and to her dad and I.

I have been repeatedly encouraged in my walk with Christ since knowing Jonathon; by witnessing this young man so faithful in the Lord who prays, not only with my daughter whom he loves so openly, but with Ed and I.

Sarah and Jon married on October 10, 2014. From my perspective their meeting was divinely orchestrated and started from their first meeting six years prior when Sarah saw his gold-coloured aura, as he walked into the Student Centre.

Early Childhood

Are they not all ministering spirits sent forth to minister for those who will inherit salvation? - Hebrews 1:14

I have frequently been the recipient of many strange, wonderful and fantastic experiences that seem so out of the ordinary that you may question my sanity or believe I am not being truthful. You would be wrong in those conclusions and I share events as I know them, have been shown them or have been told them.

I forthrightly admit I have no personal recollection of the following events in my early childhood but share this with you is as told to me by my mom and dad. I had passed my first birthday and was just beginning to walk. My mom had put me down for an afternoon nap and it got to be past the time that she would usually hear me awake in my crib. She tells me she went to my room to check on me and in her words "a monster" lay in my bed. My head was swollen and I had pinpricks of blood on my face. She said I looked like an alien. She confessed to me in the retelling that she was scared and repulsed and could not bring herself to touch me. She screamed out in fear to a boarder living at our home, Royce, to come to my room to help her. Royce picked me up, she called an ambulance and they took to me the hospital. I had septicemia, or blood poisoning.

I was in the hospital for an extended period of time, spending my second birthday there. As I understand it, I was a very sick little girl. Eventually with the grace of God I got well enough to go home. Apparently, since I was in the hospital for such a long time, I had become emotionally attached to a red-headed nurse who had been taking care of me. When the day came for me to leave the hospital, I clung to the nurse, crying not wanting to leave her and go with mom and dad. Then dad had an idea. At the time, my dad drove a refurbished, second-hand, pink Cadillac and I apparently loved the car. Dad had the nurse carry me out of the hospital and as soon as I saw the car, they tell me I let go of the nurse, scrambled into the car, and didn't look back. We went home. I have no recollection of these events at all but think it is part and parcel of the marvel of my life that God has given me. There is more to this story.

While I was in the hospital, something unusual happened. My dad, who was working, spent whatever time he could with me at the hospital. At one point I needed more treatment, perhaps blood transfusions, when he was visiting with me at the hospital. He said he was so afraid for me, as any dad would be for their sick and ailing child. My dad was not a demonstrably religious man, but he said he prayed for my recovery.

Over the years I tried to get dad to share his memory of my hospital stay because he led me to believe there was more to this story, but he never wanted to talk about it. When I was in my twenties, my dad had randomly called me one night. He had been drinking and although he wasn't a teetotaler, it was unusual for him to be intoxicated, as he seemed on the phone. He was crying and said he had something to tell me but hung up without saying what it was. For many years, whenever I asked him about it, he said to forget it because he didn't know why he called and reverted to not wanting to talk about it, which only served to pique my curiosity.

As the years passed, whenever I thought of that call the memory haunted me but I had no reason to connect it to my hospital stay. I eventually moved away, got married and started my life here in Ontario. Dad and I continued our relationship with the occasional phone call but mainly through exchanging letters. With that long ago phone call in mind, I wrote to my dad in December 2004 and asked him again about why he had called me that night. Here is what he wrote back to me in January 2005. I still have his letter and the following quote is an excerpt of my dad's words.

> 'As a small child you were in the hospital, quite sick, and although we were not allowed in the room during treatment, I was in the next part, close to yours – now this is when it becomes a dream or a vision or whatever, I am not sure, but *you came to me* and assured me that you would be alright and not to worry as you had a *friend* helping you. I do not remember seeing this friend but I had the greatest feeling of relief and calmness. A few moments later a nurse came out and told me you would be alright. I have never said this to anyone until now. I know I, at one time in your life, would have to tell you as your friend has been mine for a long time, and is still looking after you - the pact still remains. You, as any child, are blessed with the *knowledge* of all this world upon your birth and although you seem to lose it as age progresses you do not, it is still in your subconscious and in time of extreme need it will come back to you, as much as it is required at that time.
>
> It is I who made the pact so as you may be well at the time and I should have kept it to myself – now I see you are doing the deeds that was laid out for you, just live your life as good as you can. You have

no need to make me proud, I am already proud of you and my love for you.'

Although I asked him, Dad never shared with me whatever "pact" he made, who he made the pact with or any particulars of this pact. I was surprised at my dad's references to "the knowledge" and to my "friend" in his letter. I already knew about the knowledge, and as a child, I had my own special friends who impacted me in a tremendous way, which you are about to learn. *There are no coincidences in Christ.*

My wonderful dad Clyde Winsfield Shepherd passed away in his sleep in July 2020, at ninety-five years of age, a proud and decorated veteran. God was gracious in his passing.

The Seed First Planted

So then neither he who plants is anything, nor he who waters, but God who gives the increase. - 1 Corinthians 3:7

Another early experience arose as a young child. I used to be afraid of the dark. I shared my bed with my younger sister, Lynn, but once she went to sleep and I was alone, *my friends,* as I called them, would come up from behind the bed to be with me. I was visited every night by these small animal beings that were as real to me as anyone in my family was to me at that time. They did not have names, but they provided me with comfort, talked with me, and kept me company until I went to sleep.

This went on for most of my young childhood, a number of years - it seemed a very long time to my younger self. They stopped coming after my mother caught me feeding them when I was five years old.

We did not always have the luxury of having a bedtime snack. We didn't have much growing up, not through any neglect or not providing for us by our parents. There were six of us children. Mom and dad, both working, were doing their best to provide. However, on rare occasions we were fortunate enough to get a snack of a slice of bread before we went to bed. On those occasions, I would save my bread and "share" it with my friends. I would tear off small pieces of the bread and roll it between my fingers to make bread balls, and feed my friends by throwing the balls behind the bed where, in my mind, they lived.

One day, my mom was cleaning our bedroom and moved our bed out, away from the wall to find a large number of these bread balls behind my bed on the floor. The conversation went something like this:

> Mom asked me, "Child, what is this behind your bed?"
> I replied, "Bread balls."
> Mom repeated "Bread balls?"
> And I said "Yes, bread balls. They are for my friends."
> "What friends are you talking about?" asked my mom.
> "My friends that come up behind my bed to keep me company at night after Lynn goes to sleep," I replied.

It all made perfect sense to me; this was my reality. But Mom's questioning persisted "Who exactly are these friends?" I told her about the small animal beings and how they came up from behind the bed at night to keep me company, and I was sharing my bread with them. I don't know what she thought of me or my friends. My mom had the most loving heart and would never intentionally say anything to hurt me, or anyone else. She simply shook her head and kindly told me "Scherry, your friends aren't real so stop feeding them because you are making a mess."

They slowly started to leave me after I told my mom about them. I would occasionally see them but not with any regularity like before.

I was terribly saddened. We moved when I was six and unhappily for me, I never saw them at the new house, although I waited and looked for them. I missed them terribly, they had been my special friends for as long as my young mind could remember.

My mom and I never discussed my friends after that day until many years later when we would reminisce about days gone by and the funny things kids do. We'd laugh about the bread balls behind the bed. This was the earliest occasion I can recall, at five years old, when my mom first said "Child you should write a book," after she found out about my friends and the bread balls. The sub-conscious seed to write this book was first planted!

CHAPTER 3

Pain Transference

"And whatever things you ask in prayer, believing, you will receive." - Matthew 21:22

Growing up through my earlier years, my older sister Paula and her son, my nephew Bruce, lived with us. I was ten years older than he was and he was one of the cutest babies I ever saw. Bruce was the first baby that I was old enough to appreciate and love in my life.

When Bruce was about three years old, he unfortunately was plagued by toothaches and night after night I could hear him crying in pain. Nothing seemed to help. One night the pain was particularly hard on him and his crying in pain was cutting into my heart. I felt so bad for him. I understood the pain he was probably feeling because I too suffered toothaches when I was younger due to a lack of financial opportunity for my parents to send us to the dentist. Free dental care was available through our school system for families who needed it, but my older sister Karen went once and was slapped by the dentist for crying. My dad never let any of us go back.

It pained me unbearably to hear Bruce's incessant crying. As I lay in my bed, I prayed to God asking if I could take his pain for him so he could get some rest. He was so little and I felt great compassion for him. He continued to cry and I continued to earnestly pray the same prayer over and over, asking God to give me Bruce's toothache.

Some time passed. Bruce stopped crying and he fell asleep just as I was struck with the most painful toothache I had ever had. The pain lasted throughout the night and I vowed to be careful of what I prayed for in the future because I believe God answered my prayer that night and gave me Bruce's toothache pain.

That was not to be the only time I prayed for someone's pain and received it. I had headaches as a child too, not migraines but I was a worrier. As I got older, I would lie in bed and worry about many things. My folks were having problems in their relationship, we were financially disadvantaged, I worried about what was going to happen to us. I worried a lot about everything and I believe this was the reason for my headaches.

As it came to happen much later in life, my daughter Sarah had headaches. When she was a child probably about eight years old, she was awake crying one night because her head was aching. There seemed nothing I could do to relieve her pain. I gave her a cold compress and children's medicine but this headache would just not go away. In the deepest reaches of my heart, I prayed to God to give me her headache. Again, prayer after earnest prayer, I implored the Lord to give me her pain. Something miraculous happened: Sarah stopped crying and went to sleep and I immediately had the blinding, throbbing headache I believe she had been having.

It is important to understand a couple things, I have come to understand. The first is that when I initially prayed for Sarah, I did not consciously remember that I had prayed for Bruce those many years before. It wasn't until the moment I received Sarah's headache, that I remembered back to my experience with Bruce. The second and probably most important fact is that when I prayed in both these instances, I myself had previously experienced the pain for which I was praying that the other person would be relieved of. I believe that had I not known for what I was asking for, God would not have burdened me with accepting the pain of either Bruce or Sarah

Have I prayed for others since then? Of course, I have, but wonder from what spiritual depths one must honestly and earnestly desire another's pain, to be "blessed" in essentially receiving it. Pray as I might, many times over the years to accept the pain of a loved one in any circumstance, except for these two instances, has it ever happened again. I also realize that God actually let me endure the pain when I know He could have in His majesty healed them of their respective agonies. I don't know why He chose to transfer pain in these two instances, but the concept, to be careful what I pray for, was now engrained.

Prayerful Intersession

Again I say to you that if two of you agree on earth concerning anything that they ask, it will be done for them by My Father in heaven.

For where two or three are gathered together in my name, I am there in the midst of them. - Matthew 18:19-20

I have just shared that I prayed to receive other's pain on more occasions, but to no avail; the Lord in His wisdom chose to let those prayers unanswered. But He always opens a door for us. When Sarah was about two years of age, she began attending Three Little Fishes Daycare, which operated on a Christian foundation. Our older son, Michael, had also attended there, before he started grade school, and both of the children loved the staff and the atmosphere. When she was about 4 years old, I was getting her ready to leave for daycare and she told me everything was blurry. When I asked what she meant, she told me everything was fuzzy in her eyes. Upon arrival at the daycare, I relayed this to the staff and said that she was perhaps experiencing vision problems and to keep an eye on her behaviours. They advised they would watch her daily activities, especially her work-book functions. Her dad and I booked an eye examination, and sure enough, our little girl needed glasses. She didn't like to wear them, no matter how cute we told her she looked, and she *was* cute.

Every night I would read bedtime stories, first to Sarah, because she was younger, and then read to Michael after Sarah had fallen asleep. This was a nightly ritual. I would read a story; being fully animated, packed full of sounds and gestures and sometimes incorporating one of the many hand puppets our children owned. Then it was sleep time. Children being children, did not want to go to sleep and would ask for *a minute*. This involved my sitting on the side of their bed, and rubbing their backs to help them fall asleep, for just a minute, until they eventually would fall asleep. This was a special time for them, and me each night.

It was a loving custom we shared. But I noticed, as I rubbed Sarah's back, she had a bit of a bump on her back. Night after night, I noticed this bump but I did not put any thought into it and later, in retrospect, I was surprised that I had neglected it for so long. Perhaps I was in denial, but I didn't think of it as an issue, and life continued on.

The kids got older and I eventually stopped our nightly ritual. Sarah, however, loved to sleep in our bed, even when she got older. She was a chubby little girl and Ed was a big man. I slept in the middle and used to jokingly say, I was the bologna in a bologna sandwich. I loved being the bologna.

One night, I was surprised to notice that the bump on her back was still there. Ed and I decided to take her to the doctor. After a series of appointments and X-rays, we were told she had scoliosis. The doctor said it was usually hereditary. I mentioned to the doctor that I remembered my older sister Karen had one hip higher than the other. Growing up, I didn't know why; it was never talked about, nor was Karen ever treated for it to my knowledge. Maybe my parents didn't even know about it, but he confirmed in all likelihood, Karen had scoliosis. This was my first introduction to what would become the dreaded scoliosis.

The doctor gave us options on how we could proceed; first,

attempt to straighten her spine with a back brace and if that was unsuccessful, then she had to have surgery to insert rods in her back to straighten out her spine. We opted to try the brace, as the less invasive option, because the surgery could entail some pretty distressful outcomes if it was not successful. We were told Sarah could be paralyzed and lose her ability to walk; lose function of her bowels or kidneys or lose her ability to have children. These were the worst-case scenarios, but what parent wants to inflict these possibilities on their children, if other options were available.

The first brace was thick canvas, much like a corset and over a period of time, X-rays revealed that the canvas brace did not correct the problem. The second back brace, appeared to us as though it were a medieval device; heavy thick plastic fitted from a mold made from her upper body. I would strap Sarah in the best I could and then her dad would have to use his strength to close the brace. The idea was to straighten her back over time. We tried the brace for a year or so. It was heartbreaking that we had to strap her into this brace every night because it was physically painful for Sarah and emotionally painful for all of us. After a year of this torture, we came to the realization after several doctor scheduled assessments and subsequent X-rays that this brace was not working either.

We were devastated. The remaining options at this point, were to let the scoliosis take its course or have the surgery. I came to the realization that the elderly people I would see stooped, over with the large lumps on their backs, must have scoliosis. We didn't want that for Sarah's future. After much discussion and hand-wringing we decided that Sarah had to have the surgery.

The doctor said if the surgery was successful, Sarah would not have any of the aforementioned catastrophic outcomes, and she would probably gain a couple of inches in height, due her back being straightened. He assured us he would do his best to make sure she came through ok.

The surgery was scheduled just a month before Sarah's fourteenth birthday, we were terrified. I turned to God, as my last resort for my child, when now I see He should have been my first resort.

I reached out to my family, and asked them to reach out to all their prayers partners, to pray for Sarah's surgery on the scheduled date and time. Mom, and my sisters, were prayer warriors and I laid my fear in their prayerful hands, on behalf of Sarah. Everyone prayed. The ladies in the shop, where I took her to get her hair done prayed; people I worked with prayed; so many, interceded on Sarah's behalf for her surgery to be successful.

Sarah went into surgery and we waited and waited. After the sedative had worn off, we were permitted to see her. After the surgery, the doctor said we would know whether or not it had been successful by her reaction to a series of tests. The doctor came into the room and was now going to test her to ensure there was no damage to her nervous system in her legs. Praise God! Her legs reacted normally to the test, there was no nerve damage. The doctor wanted to bring her to her feet right away, and we were concerned, she had just come out of the surgery. But nurses were on either side of her, lifted her out of the bed, and brought her to her feet. Before the surgery, I was taller than Sarah, but with the help of the nurses, she slowly stood up, taller than me by about an inch and a half. I was ecstatic, the surgery was a success. God had heard all the impassioned prayers, offered up on behalf of our child, and answered them in glorious fashion!

After Sarah was home, recuperating from the surgery, I noticed she was not wearing her glasses and told her to put her glasses on. She told me she could "see." Sarah had worn glasses since she was in daycare when the doctor confirmed she needed them about ten years earlier. Because she didn't like to wear them, I assumed she just didn't want to put them on and I repeated that she should put them on. She again said, she could see. To make a long story short, I called the doctor and had her eyes tested. She was right, he said he didn't know what happened, but her vision was 20/20.

I had attributed her perfect vision to all the prayer she received when she was going into surgery and declared it a miracle. Sarah told me, however, that her vision had returned before the surgery and that she repeatedly tried to tell me but I hadn't listened. In my heart and in my mind, I still accept her renewed eyesight as a miracle, whenever her vision returned, before or after the surgery!

I continue to thank Him for His mercy, grace and loving-kindness for Sarah. God has held on to Sarah with strength that could only be imparted by His supreme majesty. In addition to what I have already shared, her headaches and scoliosis; she has had a series of medical issues, throughout her life, beginning with an umbilical hernia, that Michael, jokingly liked to poke in-and-out, because of the "squishy' sound it made. At age twelve, her tonsils and adenoids had to be removed; her right foot was fractured when she was thirteen. Surgery again, at age sixteen, for a displaced knee from dancing, one of her passions. She has vertigo, allergies and arthritis but Sarah does not let any of those things define her. She tore the tendons and broke her ankle in two places when she was twenty-seven and has experienced a number of conditions and internal issues as an adult. Through all of this, Sarah has taught me a lot about faith, by her loving and kind attitude in life; and especially her trust in God.

When Sarah was born, and even now, her left baby finger has a "pucker," at the tip. As a young child she would question me about it. I told her it was because, when she was ready to be born, she "wasn't quite done," in my belly, but she was in a hurry, and came out anyway. We still laugh about that today.

Heaven's Fragrance

For we are to God the fragrance of Christ among those who are being saved and among those who are perishing. - 2 Corinthians 2:15

As previously shared, my parents always ensured we children attend church. My sister Lynn, and brother Kevin, and I, also regularly attended Sunday school and were in the youth choir. A steady church goer, I attended my classes to prepare for and attended my Confirmation but this did not raise any particular religious feelings for me. In due course, at some point in my mid-teens, I stopped attending church. I always felt a kinship with Christ but am sad to admit I was not a frequent churchgoer after this mid-teen lapse for quite some time.

I got my first studio apartment when I was in my early twenties around 1977 and eventually moved across the street to a bigger apartment. I should have known something was out of the ordinary the day I moved in. The day before I moved, I had spent time in the apartment cleaning and painting. I didn't have much furniture at this point, but I did have my boyfriend's expensive brand-new sound system he had loaned me. I had set up the system so I could play music while I prepared the apartment to move in. As I was leaving the apartment after cleaning for the day, a man brushed past me and it was obvious he had been drinking; we did not exchange pleasantries. I briefly wondered what kind of neighbours I would have to contend with. I also had a fleeting thought whether I should go back to get the sound system but ignored the urging. It had been a long day and I was eager to get some rest.

Having already given up my apartment across the street, I had arranged with my mom to stay at her house until I was able to get my new apartment squared away. The next day, the day I was to move in, as soon as I awoke in the morning, I had an immediate sense of urgency and had a clear vision of the front door of my apartment open, having been broken into. I was beside myself with worry with no way to get there but by foot. I did not drive at the time and the apartment was not on a bus route. The whole way there I was trying to tell myself I was being ridiculous. But my mind went back to the intoxicated man I had passed as I was leaving the day before, which heightened my discomfort that was slowly growing into panic.

As I let myself into the vestibule leading to the hallway to my apartment, sure enough there it was - just as I had envisioned. My door was wide open, and worse than that, my boyfriend's new sound system was gone!! I was devastated as I would have to tell him it was stolen. As it turned out he was very understanding and did not request that I replace it for him. He was more concerned that I was safe and relieved I was not there when my apartment had been broken into. My early morning vision was the first of many strange premonitions in this apartment, and I hadn't even moved in yet!

Initially I lived there alone. My apartment was on the first floor of a very old, three-story brick building. Strange things began to manifest, such as premonitions of when the phone would ring before it did or knowing someone was at the door before they knocked, cabinet doors opening, water faucets turning on by themselves. Nothing really earth-shattering, or that scared me, more of a curiosity than anything. At least in the beginning.

Old buildings generate lots of unusual sounds in the night and I became accustomed to the sounds of the neighbours and the creaking and groaning of this old building. But there was something far more sinister I was yet to experience.

Shortly after I moved in, I lay in bed ready to go to sleep one night, I felt something hit me hard in the head. It felt like a hard kick to my temple. I was stunned by the pain. This got my attention quick. Whatever this energy was, it was negative in nature and I realized it had the potential to do me physical harm. I was alone and yes, I was scared. As always, I turned to prayer for comfort and protection, as I did this night. During my prayer, I started to drift off to sleep, I felt a body cuddle up behind me, an arm encircling me. From that night on I always felt safe alone because I knew someone or something was watching over and protecting me.

A year or so passed, life went on and Toni, my best friend at the time, moved in with me. Toni wanted to move out of her mother's house to expand her independence and we agreed to share the living expenses. We were young ladies finding our way in the world.

Toni had found and accepted the Lord shortly before she came to share the apartment with me and was encouraging me to go to church with her. Honestly, I didn't really want to go. I felt I was no stranger to Christ and, as stated, felt I had a relationship with the Lord and I often relied on prayer, so I thought it was not necessary. Toni, however, did not give up asking me, and eventually I started to regularly attend church again. Over time I eventually rededicated myself to the Lord through the reciting of the Sinner's Prayer during an altar call at the church we attended. I had reached that time in my early adult life when I was ready to commit myself to Christ.

It was while Toni and I lived at this apartment that we experienced a physical visitation by a heavenly presence. The visitation happened in the kitchen that was on the ground level, adjacent to an outside closed-in courtyard. Toni and I had just returned home after a mid-week Bible study service and our spirits were high on the Lord. We were sitting at the kitchen table talking about our Bible study and the goodness of God in our lives, sharing our blessings, when suddenly I could see light twinkling all around my peripheral vision. My vision was framed by this sparkling light, making it difficult to see clearly. As we continued to pray and praise the Lord, time appeared stop and the atmosphere became very still. The air between us began to get noticeably cloudy. I asked Toni if she could see the cloud and she affirmed that she could. Suddenly the room began to fill with the most fragrant scent of roses as we continued praising God. We knew we were being blessed by a holy presence and became quiet in reverence of it.

This spiritually precious experience was suddenly shattered by a prolonged, high-pitched, piercing scream coming directly from the other side of the kitchen window, next to where we were praying. The scream abruptly startled us out of our heavenly interlude and although we presumed it was a cat screaming outside the window, we recognized it for what it truly was. It was more than a cat - it was an evil presence enraged with the praise and worship and visitation from heaven we were experiencing inside.

Although the scream startled us, Toni and I continued in more fervent prayer. We were not to be deterred. We knew we had been privileged by experiencing a special gifting of a heavenly presence and will forever remember the power of prayer and the memorable blessing of our holy visitation.

It was after this incident that Toni and I decided to move further up the street and share my sister Karen's apartment. Her apartment was huge and easily provided room for all three of us. I called on some of our church partners to help us move. The day of the move, a church brother by the name of Buddy was struck hard on the side of his face by an unseen entity as he stepped across the threshold into my apartment. I was more than glad to be moving.

I had another glorious experience with the Holy Spirit manifesting His presence by framing my vision with dancing light, which I will share with you further on when I tell you about my friend and co-worker Jenny.

Gift of Tongues

And they were all filled with the Holy Spirit and began to speak with other tongues, as the Spirit gave them utterance. - Acts 2:4

After Toni and I moved in with Karen, the three of us were active in the Pentecostal church, attending services and doing community service. It was during this return to the church that I became more attuned to God in my life and strongly sought His direction and growth in my spiritual life.

One night on our way home from a highly-charged worship and Bible study we were on the church community bus and we were continuing in the worship and glory of God we had practiced while at the church. It was there on this bus I was first blessed with the gift of tongues. In tandem, Karen and I were speaking and appeared to be conversing in a language unknown to either of us. For me, this was a surreal experience and the beginning of my blessing of the gift of tongues, in word and song.

In this book, I will share the spiritual power of tongues, which concerned a young autistic boy at a time much later in my life.

Disillusioned

God *is* faithful, by whom you were called into the fellowship of His Son, Jesus Christ our Lord. - 1 Corinthians 1:9

A surprising, personal development occurred as I leaned into the church and the teachings of Christ. I was being convicted in my spirit over my hair. I kept my hair long and bright auburn; it was beautiful and had always been my crowning glory. However, it got to the point that, spiritually, I felt that I was being prideful and should not have this dyed bright-red hair in church. Every time I walked into the sanctuary I felt convicted by the pride of my hair, that it was holding me back from learning and prayer. How could I be humble when I was pre-occupied with my beautiful hair? I couldn't explain my inner turmoil, but I did what I thought was right - I cut my hair off to about a half an inch from my natural roots.

I felt an instant release and relief. I was so proud that I had followed the urging to be respectful to the Spirit. When I went to church the following Sunday, one of the senior church sisters, for whom I had great reverence and respect, asked me why I had cut my hair. I explained to her that I felt I was too preoccupied and prideful with loving my hair and it was causing me to be conflicted in my spirit, so I decided to rid myself of the distraction. Her response shattered me; she told me I was being ridiculous and should not have cut my pretty hair!

I was devastated and disillusioned. I slowly started to move away from the church again. In hindsight I should have known better than to listen to a word from a church member instead of the Holy Spirit who had convicted me to cut my hair. To remain honest in the telling, I used this situation to justify moving away from the church yet again. I know, I appear to have been weak and looking for any reason to go back to the world, but that is what I did.

Stranded and Lost, But Not Alone

"Fear not, for I *am* with you; Be not dismayed, for I *am* your God. I will strengthen you, Yes, I will help you, I will uphold you with My righteous right hand." - Isaiah 41:10

It wasn't long after cutting my hair that Karen, who was married but separated, was told by the church elders that she had to return to her husband. She decided to go visit him in Louisville, Kentucky. Toni and I decided to accompany her. In my heart I knew this was not a good prospect for me as I had become restless in church and was looking for a way to return to my life outside of it, in the world, and for an opportunity to let loose of the confines within the church and kick up my heels.

The three of us decided we would take the bus to Louisiana because we did not have a lot of money. I would like to say we began our trip outwardly, with good intentions. On the first leg of our trip, sometime in the middle of the night, the bus had a brief stop in Maine for a mail parcel pickup stop. It was not an intended stop for the people on the bus, but I told the bus driver I was getting off to use the washroom. Karen and Toni were sleeping, so I got off the bus to use the facilities without telling them. When I came out of the restroom and started back to the bus, I was astonished to find it had left. I was momentarily dumbfounded. Here I was, a young Black woman, alone in the middle of the night, somewhere in Maine. My purse and all my belongings were on the bus. It was 1978, we didn't carry cellphones back then, unlike common practice today. With no money and no identification, I had nothing. I was stranded!

I slowly walked back into the station, and I guess the dazed look on my face was apparent to a couple of young men sitting at the snack counter. I stammered that the bus had left me. I was confused by the sudden turn of events and I clearly didn't know what to do.

The Good Samaritans

God *is* our refuge and strength, A very present help in trouble. - Psalm 46:1

These two young men, one Black and one Caucasian, told me to come with them - they'd take me down the road to catch up with the bus. I didn't give their offer a second thought; the situation was so bizarre. I was not a blindly trusting person and fully understood the concept that bad things sometimes happened to good people. But this dark night in the middle of Maine, I wasn't thinking. I blindly followed them to their car outside and gratefully got in the back seat. They started down the road the bus had travelled.

These young men were very nice and polite towards me. They asked me where I was from and where I was going and we made general small talk. I was totally oblivious to the potential harm I had placed myself in by trusting these two men. As I sat in the back seat watching the road ahead of us between their heads up front, it wasn't so long before I saw the bus heading toward us in the distance. I yelled out to the driver "That's the bus!" He immediately began to flash his lights and honk his horn to get the bus driver's attention.

The bus stopped and I expressed my sincere gratitude to these two young men. Whatever would I have done without them. To this day I still wonder. They said they were happy to help, wished me well, and drove away, just like that.

I gladly reunited with my sister and friend and I got back on the bus. I came to find out that since Karen and Toni were still asleep when I got off the bus, they hadn't initially understood that I was not on the bus when it pulled out. It wasn't long, however, before Karen was awoken by the Holy Spirit to find I was not with her. She asked Toni if I was sitting with her and when Toni said I was not, they determined I was not on the bus with them. Karen demanded that the driver turn around to go back for me. He gladly turned back around, probably fearing any potential repercussions he could have faced had he kept on going without me. Karen was incensed at what she felt was his negligence, but it was not his fault, simply an unfortunate occurrence.

When I got back on the bus, I relayed to Karen and Toni what had transpired from the time I left the bus to use the washroom, to my triumphant return. In the telling of my misadventure, I realized how truly fortunate I was. Any number of terrible things could have happened to me that night with these young men. No one would have known what happened to me, no one would have known when I got off the bus and with whom I had left the snack bar. These young men *just happened* to be sitting at the snack bar, were sufficiently concerned for my plight, offered to chase down the bus, took a total stranger out in the middle of the night alone and did not harbour any ill will toward me or display ulterior motives. By their actions they became my guardian angels. God knew what was going to *just happen* and orchestrated my well-being.

Karen led Toni and I in prayer of thankfulness for my safe protection and return. We recognized that God sent angels to watch over me, and I have to believe I was the recipient of His divine, watchful eyes that night. Those young men were His agents and were sent to deliver me out of harm's way.

Thank You Father God.

Dancing with the Devil

Where can I go from Your Spirit? Or where can I flee from Your presence? If I ascend into heaven, You *are* there; If I make my bed in hell, behold, You *are there*. - Psalm 139:7-8

The rest of the bus trip was uneventful until we got to New York for a stop-over. Toni and I wanted to get out from under the watchful eye of Karen and, to be truthful, God. The stories Karen told us about Louisville, seemed to suggest that we were headed to a sleepy, boring, country setting. Toni and I decided that, instead of transferring to Louisville to continue our original plan, we would instead transfer over to Philadelphia. Toni's ex-husband lived in Philadelphia, and we figured we could have a better time if we went there instead. Karen was not pleased with our decision, but she went on to Louisville while Toni and I went to Philadelphia.

This was not one of my best decisions but a reflection of the God we serve, even as we try to abandon Him. Even after His mercy in delivering me from evil in Maine, I had much yet to learn about His goodness and His grace.

Toni and I were quick to get back to partying and the life in the world when we got to Philadelphia. One late night, driving home after being out, Toni and her husband were in the back seat and one of her husband's friends was driving with me in the front seat. It was dark and raining but not so bad that we couldn't see. As we were driving along, we were coming to a construction median, set up in the middle of the road ahead of us. I could clearly see it and there was no question in my mind that the driver could see it as well. As we got closer to the construction, he did not attempt to move away from the median. I thought he was just playing chicken with me and trying to scare me so I remained quiet as he got closer and closer to it. The next thing I knew, he hit the median and the car launched into the air. I don't think I had time to scream; I was in shock. The car went airborne, flew about five car lengths, and jarringly landed on all four wheels.

We all were jolted when the car landed, and we got out of the car to see what happened and assess the damage. There was none, not a scratch. The car, even the glass in the windows, was intact. Toni and her husband were firing questions at his friend and I. "What happened? What did we hit?" His friend said he didn't know what happened. I told them about the construction median and how I thought he was going to veer away from it as we got closer. They looked back in amazement to see the median I told them we had hit and subsequently, airborne, flew over. The friend said he didn't see it until that moment when he looked back at it. We couldn't believe how far the car had travelled and that we were all miraculously safe, not so much as a scratch, on any one of us or the car!

I realized that although we had tried to run from God by going to Philadelphia and dancing with the devil, He kept His hand on us and kept us safe when we did not deserve His protection, His mercy, His grace, or His loving-kindness. How great is our God! I felt the enemy had tried to destroy Toni and I in this accident. I now had a deeper understanding of God's faithfulness and knew He would never leave me.

I wish I could say I ran back to the church after this frightening incident, but sadly it took quite some time and a devastating, life-altering tragedy for me to again seek His divine love and forgiveness which I will share a while later.

CHAPTER 4

A Destiny Fulfilled

A man's steps *are* of the Lord; How then can a man understand is own way? - Proverbs 20:24

My husband Ed and I first met in early 1979 in my home town of Saint John, New Brunswick. We had several encounters that I did not initially recall, so my timing may be a bit off. After we were married, he reminded me of the earlier occasions that we had encountered each another, and I remembered each occasion but did not realize it was him I had interacted with until he reminded me of our numerous chance encounters. Sarah and Jon experienced the same disconnect at their first encounters in 2008, as Ed and I had back in 1979.

    I thought I had first met Ed one evening when I was out with one of my girlfriends at a local social establishment. I had gone to the washroom and as I exited, a tall good-looking man addressed me by name, surprising me by his greeting. Where I was from, eligible young Black men were not in abundance. When Ed called my name, he was standing in front of an open doorway, framed by the light behind him, highlighting his six-foot, five-inch outline. *Wow,* I thought! He invited me to join his group at their table. I did briefly sit with him and his friends but eventually returned to where my friends were seated. Throughout the night as the evening progressed, we talked and danced. As the end of the evening started to wind down, my brother Kevin invited a number of people to his home to continue the fun and revelry. Ed asked me if I wanted to ride with him to Kevin's, but I told him I had come with friends and the girl code was to leave with the friends you came with. But I said I would see him later at Kevin's.

As it turned out, unbeknownst to me, the friend I had travelled out with, had also met Ed previously that evening. Unaware of their meeting, I shared with her he had asked me if I wanted him to drive me to the party but I chose to leave with her because it was the girls' rule. I thought when she and I left, we were headed to Kevin's, but to my surprise she drove me directly home. I lived some distance from Kevin's house, and by the time she dropped me off at my house it was late. I decided to stay home and go to bed rather than make my way to the party. My sister Lynn, who had gone to the party told me later that Ed had been watching and looking for me, but eventually he had to leave to go back to work, disappointed I hadn't shown up.

I didn't see Ed for quite some time after this. He simply disappeared. I found no one, except Lynn, who remembered him, and not a soul knew where he went. Lynn's boyfriend actually knew Ed but wanted to deflect my attention and told me his name was Joe. I knew his name was not Joe and ignored his attempts to throw me off track. He did this, I later found out, because he didn't want Ed and I to get together. He knew Ed and wanted him to remain a "single" man so they could hang out together, therefore he wouldn't divulge any information to identify Ed to me.

Ed remained among the missing. I had started a new job shortly after returning home from Philadelphia and became particularly close with a new work friend named Sue. I couldn't get Ed off my mind and was telling her about him and how I was enamored with him and that he seemed to have disappeared. She listened but had no solutions to offer and time went on.

One day I unexpectedly got flowers delivered for the first time ever, and before reading the card, I immediately knew they were from Ed. Shortly after, I got a phone call from him asking if I would like to meet up. Of course, I did. I had been waiting for him to resurface for quite some time and I told him so. It turned out that Ed was a marine engineer and had returned to his job on the sea for three months, which is why he seemed to have disappeared. He did, however, know Kevin but didn't know that Kevin and I were related. When he returned from his recent voyage, he went to see Kevin to ask about me, knowing I was supposed to show up for Kevin's party months earlier. Upon hearing his description of me, Kevin told him, "That's my sister." He asked Kevin for my address and phone number and that is how he sent the flowers and then called me.

We started to date, and on one occasion he told me he wanted me to meet his best friend and his best friend's wife. He arranged for us to go to their house in the country one day, and I was excited to meet and get to know his friends. How utterly flabbergasted we all were as I entered their home to find that my new work colleague, in whom I had confided in all those months, telling her all about the man who I met who had gone missing, was his *best friend's wife*, Sue! Neither she nor I had ever had any inkling that my tall, dark, missing stranger was *her* husband's best friend. We were all amazed at the coincidence.

Eventually Ed and I decided to move in together. We then talked of marriage and decided to elope to Toronto. It had always been my dream to elope - I thought it would be so romantic - and Ed agreed to start our future life together this way. We planned we would make the move when his next work term at sea came around. This would give me time, three months, to go to Toronto, initially stay with a friend, look for a job, and scope out the apartment availability awaiting his next furlough.

Through God's grace and favour, exactly one month of arriving in Toronto, I found a great job at Centennial College, Ontario's first community college, starting on October 6, 1980. I retired from the college in September 2020 after 40 years of employment, fully aware and appreciative of how good God has been to me throughout my professional life. He opened doors and provided opportunities that only He can manifest.

When Ed returned to Toronto after his work schedule was over, he proposed – he asked me to marry him - and I said yes. Again, I admit I was still not attending church and neither was my friend I had been staying with. Ed and I did some research, through the Yellow Pages, there was no internet, and found a minister. We made the arrangements, got our marriage license and went to the minister's home to be married. We did not have a circle of friends to stand up and witness our marriage except my girlfriend so we asked her and her then boyfriend to witness our union. They agreed but the day Ed and I were to get married, my girlfriend had an argument with her boyfriend, who was supposed to stand up with us, and she came to our wedding with a total stranger. Ed and I got married November 15, 1980. We haven't seen the stranger since!

Once Ed and I were married, we found our own apartment and started our life together as man and wife. He eventually had to return to duty for his marine engineer job for three months and left provision for me to be financially comfortable in his absence. Our apartment, however, proved to be unsuitable and we agreed I would find another apartment while he was away. I found one across the street from where we lived by the time he returned. However, as we settled into our lives, Ed decided he didn't want to return to the life on the sea and we decided to start a family.

Being married gave Ed and I lots of time to talk and reminisce about our first meeting. This is when I was surprised to find out that I had actually met Ed before my first remembrance of the night at the social club. Ed reminded me of a party we had attended together where he had introduced himself to me but had to leave the party to get back to the ship for his work shift. I remembered the party and I remembered a young man I had been speaking to who had to leave. I did not know that it had been Ed.

He reminded me of another meeting; one afternoon when my sister and I were walking through Saint John's uptown King's Square and we came upon him sitting on a bench reading. He said hello to us as we passed. I remembered this encounter because at the time we didn't know who he was, and everyone Black knew everyone else who was Black in the city. I recall he was dressed in overalls and his hair was styled in natty dreadlocks, unusual at the time back then. As we passed him sitting on the bench, I was unimpressed by his clothing choice as well as his hair style, and I made a comment to my sister. She prophetically replied "Girl, that could be your future husband." Who would have thought her correct at the time?

Through all the mysterious chance encounters I didn't remember; the night at the party, the attempts of friends to keep us apart, Ed being friends with my brother, my work confidante being Ed's best friend's wife, my sister's premonition, and our best man being replaced by a stranger, it appears there was a destiny to be fulfilled. Ed and I celebrated our fortieth wedding anniversary in November 2020 and are still going strong for a higher purpose, yet to be revealed.

After Ed and I married, we moved several times, each time to better neighbourhoods as we started to raise our children. First, Michael was born in 1982 and then Sarah came in 1988. After Michael was born, we had moved into a brand-new townhouse development. At the time we were still renters, but it had a back yard and more room for Michael to run and play and the extra bedroom for when Sarah was born. Unfortunately, the neighbourhood started to deteriorate by the time Michael was twelve and Sarah six. We started to hear gunshots at night and decided it was time to find and purchase our own home and to get the children out of this declining environment.

In 1995 we purchased our home in a nearby Ajax suburb community and expected to live happily ever after. It was not to be.

Ghostly Visitor

Vindicate me, O Lord, For I have walked in my integrity. I have also trusted in the Lord; I shall not slip. - Psalm 26:1

As stated, we moved into our current home in July 1995. We have a visiting ghost or some may say a spirit. At least we *had* a ghost, as no one has seen her in a while. Sarah told me about her before I had my own first sighting. Our visitor appears to be a little blond girl about seven years old.

Sarah was also about seven at the time she first told me about the little girl visitor. Sarah repeatedly told me she would see a little blond girl's reflection staring out at her from the brass doorknob of her bathroom. This sounded as bizarre to me then as it does to you now. I initially put it down to an overactive imagination - that is until I had my own encounters.

It was a couple of years before I first encountered this apparition. I was coming home from work, and as I put the key in the lock to enter my front door, through the beveled glass, on the top half of the door, I saw this little blond girl with a pony-tail in the foyer on the other side of the door. Naturally I was surprised that someone was in the house; nobody should have been at home, least of all a little blond stranger. As I opened the door, the little girl ran away from me and I chased her. I could see the pony-tail ahead of me.

The layout of our first floor allows for a continuous circular path from the foyer, through the hall, through the kitchen, through the dining room, through the living room leading back to the foyer. We have home security and the alarm suddenly went off. I was so busy trying to catch up with her little blond pony-tail, always a step ahead around the circular bend, I had forgotten to turn off the home security alarm. Yet, she was nowhere to be found. The fact that the alarm had not sounded with her in the house before I arrived was also an indication that this was no ordinary intruder. Now I realized this was the little girl Sarah had been telling me about.

My second sighting was perhaps a year or so later. I had just purchased a matching bedding set for our bedroom. It was quite lovely, with a bed-skirt, matching pillow cases and comforter. Honestly, I had never before owned something quite so fancy for my bedroom. I made up the bed to surprise Ed when he came home from work and then went downstairs to cook dinner. A few moments later, I went back upstairs to retrieve something and there she was - the little blond girl - laying on my new comforter, with her head resting on my pillow. Only for a split second did I see her but there she was, unmistakably lying on the bed, enjoying the comfort of the new bed coverings.

That was my last sighting of the little blond girl, but Sarah encountered her one last time after this sighting, which I will later share.

Lifted by Angels

In *their* hands they shall bear you up, Lest you dash your foot against a stone. - Psalm 91:12

Ed and I were attending an out-of-town work function held by the company he worked with. He was receiving an award for his many contributions to the organization. The event was a lovely affair with Ed receiving recognition and many accolades for the impacts he had made on the organization. I was proud to be there to support him and witness the recognition of his achievements.

The celebratory tone of the night was shattered when, after the function, we returned to our hotel room to a message saying I should call my family in Saint John. We had left our hotel contact information with our babysitter at home, but the message was to call my sister Karen in Saint John. Something had to be wrong.

I tentatively dialed the number, not knowing what I was going to hear. I was devastated when I learned my oldest sister Paula, who was not yet even yet fifty years old, had passed away of a sudden heart attack earlier that day. I was struck with a sense of loss, but also a sense of detachment at the time because I was away from home in unfamiliar surroundings, had just returned from the award festivities, and just feeling this unexpected news could not be true. It was unbelievable, but turned out to be sadly, very real.

Ed and I returned to our home the next morning, and after much discussion, we decided that I would return home to Saint John alone to attend my sister's funeral and represent our family.

It was during this visit to Saint John, in March 1996, that the most extraordinary occurrence happened. Paula's funeral had not yet taken place and there were many family members congregated at Paula's house. We were in the basement visiting and reminiscing about Paula. She was a warm, wonderful God-fearing woman, one who would literally give you the shirt off her back. But our dear sister, daughter, mother, aunt and friend - Paula - had a hilarious side to her nature and we were all sharing personal funny stories with each other, and there were many. There wasn't a dry eye in the house, not for crying from sadness, but from laughter and joy. The mood was humourously charged and highly elevated with the hilarious stories everyone had to tell.

At one point during the evening, I decided to go upstairs to get some refreshments. On my way back down the basement stairs, which were rather steep, I could not believe what happened. Although I was being careful, as I descended the very top of the staircase, the heel of one of my boots caught on the step, plunging me into a headlong fall. I had a split-second thought that I would end up lying at the bottom of the stairs badly broken and hurt. Suddenly, I felt something lifting me up, supporting both arms from behind. My feet were thrashing in the air one moment, and the next moment I was gently set down on the next step, totally composed and in full possession of my balance!

It was incredulous that my fall had been interrupted, and I knew I had been saved by an unseen entity or entities, later confirmed to me to be actual angels. Then in my spirit I softly heard, *This is not about you.* I instinctively realized that, had I fallen, the conversation and attention would have deflected away from Paula's remembrances and goodness and all the love and laughter she brought into the world. Had I continued to fall, the conversation and attention would have shifted to be about me lying at the bottom of the stairs, hurt, or even worse.

Paula was a child of God and this moment of love and remembrance was not to be denied her. Because I was lifted up by unseen hands, memories of Paula continued to be shared, be revealed, retold and warmly relished by the family and everyone in attendance.

I believe God honoured Paula's memory and her love for Him by allowing everyone to love and remember her without disruption or distraction. Miraculously, at the same time, I was saved from whatever nasty outcome had been waiting for me at the bottom of the stairs. God's mercy is undeniable.

Lucid Dreams

Blessed *is* the man who endures temptation; for when he is approved, he will receive the crown of life which the Lord has promised to those who love Him. - James 1:12

I have experienced a number of lucid dreams in my life. Some were induced; some were not. It is important to first set the stage to understanding what precipitated my lucid dreaming to begin with. As I was growing up, some of my friends referred to me as Miss Goody Two-Shoes Scherry Shepherd. I felt I was teased because I followed rules at home and at school, and yes, I was a good girl. I am not a psychologist, but I am sure that my first instances of lucid dreams would be in response to repressed thoughts and actions.

While growing up, there was a small corner store, Bessie's, at the top of the street where we lived. This store had penny-candy displayed in boxes at eye level, to entice the neighbourhood kids, myself included. Most of us we did not have lots of money, so the opportunity to buy candy came only once a week when we received our allowance or if we occasionally found pop bottles that we could redeem for pennies. The allowance did not last long, and then we had to wait for the next week to splurge on some candy unless we were lucky to find the occasional pop bottle.

Some of the kids in the neighbourhood would not wait for their weekly allowance or did not receive a weekly allowance and would sometimes go to the store to steal the candy. I was too afraid to do this because if I had gotten caught stealing, I'm not sure what my parents would have done. Also, I did not want to embarrass or shame them, through any actions I took. But, at the same time, I was jealous of the kids who would steal and thus have the candy reward. I wanted the candy but was not prepared to chance getting caught and having my folks find out. My first experience of lucid dreaming surrounded this experience, and then variations of this dream recurred throughout my childhood.

My first lucid dream found me standing at the bottom end of the street when I realized I was, in fact, asleep. My first thought upon this awareness was that Bessie's store, on the corner, had all this candy. I realized in the dream that if I stole some candy and I got caught, all I had to do was wake up and there would be no punishment, no repercussions. With this awareness in mind, I would begin to walk quickly toward the store with the intent to steal some candy. I never made it. Each time I had this particular lucid dream I would wake up before I reached the store. I never did get to steal the candy in these dreams, not once!

When I got older, I developed a process to try to induce lucid dreams. I loved my dream life. Since I was a child, I used to have fantastic wonderful dreams and wanted to experience more lucid dreams. So, I started this ritual in which I randomly asked myself, *Am I awake or am I asleep?* After many months of asking this question when I was awake, finally, one night when I was asleep, I asked the question and realized I was in fact dreaming. It worked! My persistence paid off! I was much older by this time and I was long past thinking about the candy store. I decided to fly. Away I went in my dream flying all around. But I could not sustain the dream; I woke up before I could fly to a specific place or destination.

I was never able to induce a lucid dream on demand, only when I employed my process through asking myself the question and lucked into being asleep when I asked myself. The random lucid dreams I had over the years were few and far between. I could not sustain them; upon realizing I was in a lucid dream I could feel myself begin to wake up. Later on in time, a different lucid dream had me in a snow storm and I was walking between two building in my home town. I realized I no longer lived there and so I must be dreaming, and if I was dreaming, I did not have to walk in the snow storm. This realization prompted me to fly up over the building to get out of the storm. I was elated upon waking that I had been able to direct that dream.

I also had lucid dreams, or rather nightmares, where I was flying and being chased by monsters and demons, but I never got caught by them. Disconcertingly, it was decidedly harder to wake myself up out of these bad dreams. Many times, it seemed like the entities were laughing and mocking me because I couldn't wake up and it took great fortitude to extract myself from those terrifying lucid episodes.

One vivid lucid dream is burned into my psyche forever.

As many young couples sometimes experienced, raising a young family made life seem difficult some days. Juggling the responsibilities of demanding and conflicting work schedules - Ed worked nights, I worked days - and our attempts to maintain a thriving household, organize and sustain individual child care for our two children, sometimes stretched our abilities and our finances. One of my household tasks was to organize our family budget and I suggest that particular task may have precipitated this startling dream.

In the dream, I met a tall, handsome and very wealthy man who adored me. He lived in an enormous, opulent big white mansion and wanted me to be with him forever, and love him as much as he loved me. It was tempting, but I told him I knew I was dreaming. I asked him, "How could it happen? How could I be with you?" He told me I could stay with him simply by entering the mansion with him. All I had to do was agree to stay and step into the mansion and I would not wake up. I understood this to mean I would die in my sleep and not return to my life as I knew it. I asked about my waking life and the snare was revealed – of course, I could not have anyone come with me. I would have to leave my family and my life, as I knew it, behind!

I remember standing at the front door of his mansion, he stood in the doorway holding my hand and waiting for me to enter. Was it wrong to feel so tempted, to feel the adoring love of a rich man, to be free of the financial challenges and the day-to-day family responsibilities? I don't know if it was wrong to feel tempted, but in my heart the temptation was not strong enough. I just couldn't and wouldn't leave my family. I told him "No, I couldn't stay." He stood in the doorway, sadly watching me as I stepped back, away from him, away from the mansion.

I woke up shaken by the paradoxical implications of the dream. Was the dream a real experience? Did I really have a choice? What would have happened had I chosen to stay and walked into the mansion with him? Would I really have passed away in my sleep? If not, would I have awoken to experience a lifetime of internal guilt and regret knowing that provided with an opportunity, I would have chosen riches over my family? Only God knows the answers.

I am forever grateful for the love of my family I felt in my heart to draw me back. I have never regretted awakening to my real life and the real challenges and real responsibilities that went with it. That is life, after all. My desire to persevere in the here and now, despite challenges, demonstrates my inner value placed in life, commitment to family and most of all - to and for - love. We live, we love, we learn and we grow.

After taking time to reflect I have felt that this dream was a divine test of my spirit, a test to determine where my heart and desires truly lay. I am thankful the prospect of riches did not cause me turn my back on my family and my life. By the grace of God and the spirit He instilled in me, I believe love passed this ultimate test.

God Was Calling Me

Now then, we are ambassadors for Christ, as though God were pleading through us: we implore *you* on Christ's behalf, be reconciled to God. - 2 Corinthians 5:20

God was attempting to call me back to church fellowship since I left in 1978, but I was resistant to the recommitment of declaring my life as His. His overwhelming love for me was not discouraged by my lack of reciprocation. He persisted by sending a holy messenger who was diligent in her attempts to see me embrace the Lord as strongly as she did.

It started in March 2001. My son Michael had a part-time job at a local fast-food restaurant. Like many young people he could thereby arrange to pay for his stylish lifestyle; clothes, shoes, music, and let us not forget, girls. One day I went to pick him up from work and didn't see him waiting for me, as he usually did, inside the restaurant. I attempted to catch the attention of several young clerks at the counter to inquire where he was and was being soundly ignored. There were no other customers at the counter and I was about to interrupt their personal conversation when, from the far end of the counter, a more mature female employee with a big smile began waving at me to come to her for assistance. She was very pleasant and when she found out I was there to see Michael, she kindly said she would go find him for me. When Michael and

I were on our way home, I asked him about her, what she was like and her name. He told me her name was Judy and she was a really, really special lady.

Even in the short interaction I had with Judy, I had been impressed by her customer service, her pleasant demeanour, her maturity and willingness to help me when the others had been ignoring me. I thought to myself she would make a great addition to my work staff, specifically for those reasons. I was employed in the student financial aid college sector and the students we served often needed our compassion, empathy and patience in dealing with their challenging issues. All these characteristics appeared to be inherent in Judy's presentation of service, and she would be an asset to our department. Most of my staff were younger, and although very competent in their day-to-day dealings with our students, I felt they could improve their portfolios by fostering a warm component to their interactions with our students that Judy could model.

At the time, my position at the college allowed me to hire part-time workers when a vacant position arose without undergoing a lot of human resource technicalities and it just so happened (nothing "just so happens" with God) that I had a part-time position to fill.

I felt compelled to hire her; she seemed special in some way. After giving it some thought for a couple of days, I went back to the restaurant to speak with her. I didn't see her at the counter, and again I had to make my presence known to the staff behind the counter who, once more, appeared to be more interested in their private conversations. When finally acknowledged, I asked if a lady named Judy was working that day. One young lady said she was not in that day and asked what she could do for me. Not divulging my reason, I told her I needed to speak with Judy and would come back another day as it was a personal matter.

The following day I returned again and asked for Judy and someone went to get her. I expect that her co-worker had told her that I had been there previously asking for her. When Judy came out from the back, I asked her if we could we talk a moment, and she looked a bit concerned of why I would want to speak with her. I reminded her that I was Michael's mom and that she had spoken with me several days before. I could see her relax a bit but I could tell she was still hesitant.

Talking with her, I shared how impressed I was with the interaction we had on that first day. I told her that I believed she would be an asset to my department, and explained the work we did and how her maturity and obvious desire to assist someone would be beneficial. I asked if she would consider coming to work with me at the college. Judy was so surprised that I was offering her a position. I quickly gave her my college business card so she would know I was sincere and making a legitimate offer. Judy appeared to be a bit flustered and told me she was flattered that I thought of her that way, but was not sure she could do the job and she would need to go home and discuss it with "her handsome husband Jim." Over the ensuing years, I came to hear that wonderful phrase of endearment regarding her husband from Judy on a consistent basis. I assured Judy she would have complete training and left her to discuss it with Jim.

I was not privy to the conversation that took place between Judy and Jim, but I thought luck was on my side when Judy accepted the job and began working with me in 2001. But it wasn't luck on my side. As I came to find out, it was God reaching out to me.

This was the beginning of the Lord calling me back to Him. I should have listened. I had plenty of opportunity working with Judy, who proudly carried her love of Christ on her sleeve. She loves the Lord and was constantly encouraging me to come to her church or to speak with her and her handsome husband Jim about spiritual issues I was dealing with as we talked often about God and His touch on our respective lives. People couldn't help but love Judy; she was so honest and open in her love of Christ, and we formed what I believe was a wonderful relationship. But I still wasn't listening to His invitation to return to His house of worship through her persistent urging.

We had many warm conversations concerning Christ, and I had

shared my former organized-religion experiences and commitments. Sadly, I didn't respond to her many requests to come to her church, although she was relentless in her attempts for me to join her. I always told her I didn't need to go to church because I had "a relationship with Christ in my heart." I always honestly felt I did have a strong relationship with Christ, and I knew He would always hold on to me, in part due to the many past experiences I had already had, but at the time I didn't see the need to go to church or, more importantly, even question why He was trying to call me back. I told her I would go back when the time was right. If only I had known then that God, in His infinite mercy was calling me, through Judy, to come home to Him before tragedy would strike my life.

Though heart-breaking tragedy was yet to come for me and my family, my God and Saviour continued in His ultimate mercy held on to me with His nail-pierced hands. He steadfastly holds on to me every day I draw breath.

Thank You precious Lord for not giving up on me and carrying me through the fire that was yet to come.

Divine Intervention

And let us not grow weary while doing good, for in due season we shall reap if we do not lose heart. - Galatians 6:9

"I wasn't afraid; it had to be divine intervention." That is what I told the reporters who interviewed me on the occasion that I and another person helped an elderly couple out of their home which was enveloped in smoke, earning us each a Community Member Award from the Toronto Police Services Board.

I worked as the Student Financial Services Manager at the college at the time, and the week prior to the first day of fall classes I experienced what I considered the most challenging engagement of my professional career. I was responsible for the disbursement and distribution of thousands of government loans to students anxious to get their semester started. Students had arrived en masse, far exceeding our service preparations and prompting a student, or students, to call the media. This action prompted a community news article about the long lineups and student frustrations at the college. This occurrence happened long before we could utilize direct deposit to disburse students' financial aid directly into their bank accounts. Students had to arrive in person, present appropriate identification, pay tuition fees and have courses confirmed prior to their loans being released to them. The Ontario Student Loan Program (OSAP) loan disbursement process at that time was a labour intensive manual process; one student at a time. Due to the large number of students who showed up expecting to pick up their loans that day, numbers that far exceeded our capacity, it was not an exaggeration to say it turned into a logistical nightmare. The students came to Progress campus, our largest campus, and it wasn't pretty. The media attention did not look good on the college, my department or more pointedly – me! The responsibility for this debacle lay squarely on my shoulders. I was professionally mortified.

My dedicated staff and I worked tirelessly, working through the crush and we finished out the week in good stead. However, we had three more campuses, and we were scheduled to start releasing loans to all those students the beginning of the following week. My biggest concern was for our then second largest campus, Warden Woods. I needed to ensure the distribution of loans went more smoothly than it had the week before at the at the main Progress campus. In order to satisfy student expectations, provide support to my staff and keep our college away from any further negative press, I felt I had to personally visit the Warden campus to oversee the loan disbursement operation.

On the morning on September 3, 2003, I set off for the Warden campus after first visiting the Progress main campus to ensure that process was going smoothly. Once I was comfortable that everything was in order at the Progress campus, I set out in my car, heading toward the Warden campus.

It was a refreshing September day, bright and crisp. I drove off the 401 Highway and continued down Warden Avenue toward the campus and came to a red light and stopped. Waiting at the light I noticed, what I first thought was steam from the air vent, billowing up from the side of a house as though someone was doing laundry this early morning. With the potential challenge waiting for me ahead at the Warden campus of frustrated students and line-ups, I absently thought to myself, if I could be home, I wouldn't be doing laundry at that time of the morning, I would be sleeping. I don't know what prompted me to do so, but at this moment I rolled down my window, and before I could drive off, I smelled smoke! I realized that what I had thought was laundry room steam billowing out of the vent and up the wall, wasn't steam from the laundry but it was smoke. The house was on fire!

The light turned green and instead of continuing to the campus I turned my car into the driveway of the house. I was sure someone else could smell it too and would follow me but that didn't happen. I ran up the half dozen stairs to the front door and surprisingly found it was unlocked. I opened the door and smoke came flooding out. I peeked inside and could see a form and I yelled for the person to come out. The person didn't respond. I yelled again, and again no response. I knew I had to go in and I did something I have since found out is *not* what you should do in a fire. The smoke was so black I wanted to be able to find my way out so I propped the door open with a garden chair that was sitting there on the front porch.

I ran into the house towards the form I could make out through the smoke. When I reached it, I found it was an elderly lady and I told her "We have to leave, there is a fire". I had turned 50 that May and had prided myself on my physical strength, as I worked out regularly and power-walked daily. This lady was elderly, and rather portly, but I couldn't move her, I couldn't get her out on my own. She refused to budge and the smoke was getting thicker. She kept repeating what I thought was *cat*. So, I lied - I told her once we got outside, I would go back for the cat, having no intention of going back in the house once we got out. It didn't help, she wouldn't move and I couldn't move her!

I knew I couldn't get this lady out on my own. I had no other option so I ran outside to get help. I ran down the stairs and into the street. Cars were driving around me and I guess I looked a bit frantic, a Black lady yelling for help in a predominantly Caucasian neighbor, in the middle of the road early in the morning. No one would stop, and one man actually rolled up his car window in my face when I approached his car. As I was running from car to car, desperately seeking someone to help, I saw someone had pulled into the driveway of the house and I ran back to meet up with him.

I breathlessly told this young man there was a lady in the house and I couldn't move her to get her out. We ran up the stairs, he was in front of me and I kept pushing him ahead of me on the stairs, into the house, and down the hallway because I had been inside and knew where she was. I don't know what he must have been thinking. I am not sure at this point he knew what was going on but he was there to help. When we reached her, he told her we had to leave, and again she repeated "cat'" and refused to move. Just then, the young man saw another figure in a bedroom off the hallway, and he told me to go get that person and he would take the lady out. Once she saw that we were going to help the other person, who turned out to be her husband, we were able to lead them both out safely.

Neighbours had arrived by now, and someone called 911. The neighbours got them both chairs and blankets and made the elderly couple comfortable as they waited for the fire department. The neighbours told us they did not speak English and that is why we could not communicate with them. In hindsight I think the lady was saying *can't* rather than cat, trying to say that she couldn't leave because her husband was in the back bedroom. I had a brief discussion with the police officer who had arrived, gave him my name and told that I had to leave to get to work at the college. I then left immediately to take care of my student loan disbursement operation at the Warden campus, still a few kilometers down the road.

I went on to work and the rest of the day was a blur of students and taking care of their financial aid issues, which seemed like minor issues compared to running into what I thought, was a burning building. I was elated and over the moon with emotion. I knew this young man and I had performed a good deed in assisting this elderly couple. I later learned the name of the young man who had accompanied me on this mission, was John. I also learned that the house had not been engulfed in a raging fire, rather, a fire had started in a piece of furniture, which had caused the billows of black smoke throughout the house.

When I got home and shared my story, my husband was uneasy out of concern for my well-being, that I had potentially risked my life, but my children were exceptionally proud of their mother, unaware of the danger.

I thought that was the end of it, but as it turned out, Danny, the Police Sergeant who attended, was a friend of a colleague at the college, named Joe, and through him got my contact information. I understand it was this sergeant who contacted a number of community news outlets and subsequently a number of articles were written on what had transpired that morning. I was happy to share my part in this story with the media, especially after the bad press the week before, plus I was pretty proud of the role I played.

"Divine intervention led heroes to fire rescue" read one of the headlines in the Scarborough Mirror on September 12, 2003. It was attributed to my comment "I wasn't afraid; it had to be divine intervention." I certainly did attribute the saving of these people to divine intervention for a number of reasons. I feel God set the stage to help these people long before the event took place. If I hadn't had the horrible work experience the week before, I would not have driven to the Warden campus on this particular day. I don't know what prompted me to roll down my window as I waited for the light. I don't know what prompted this young man to drive into the driveway to help, but without his assistance, who knows how this may have ended for this elderly couple.

God works in mysterious ways. Through His divine interventions He orchestrated the saving of this elderly couple long before John and I got there that crisp September morning.

A Celebration

This *is* the day the Lord has made; We will rejoice and be glad in it. - Psalm 118:24

Many accolades from helping this couple out of their home, culminated with an invitation to attend an award presentation event with the Toronto Police Services Board in 2004. My family - Ed, Michael, Sarah and Kevin - accompanied me to this event. Many people in the community were being recognized for various selfless acts and I was so proud to be a included in this celebrated group. Ed was still a bit unsettled but he, Michael, Sarah and Kevin, were proudly there to celebrate with me.

A Toronto Police Service photographer was there to take pictures of the participants and family members to commemorate the evening. The photographer took several pictures of my family and I as I held my framed award. We were standing alongside then Chief of Police Julian Fantino and Toronto Police Services Board Vice-Chair Pam McConnell.

Michael asked the photographer to specifically take a picture with just him, Chief Fantino, Vice-Chair McConnell, and I. It was so sweet, Michael leaned down and kissed me on the cheek just as the picture was taken. This was an unforgettable celebration that had taken place in the Grand Foyer of the Toronto Police Headquarters on College Street in Toronto.

Another unforgettable event was to take place in the Grand

Foyer Toronto Police Headquarters on College Street in Toronto that would serve to alter my life forever, which you will learn about later.

Deliverance from Danger

And the Lord will deliver me from every evil work and preserve *me* for His heavenly kingdom. To Him *be* glory forever and ever. Amen! - 2 Timothy 4:18

Many of you have probably experienced that "little voice" that speaks unexpectedly to you, which prompts you to do a certain thing or follow a certain path for which you have no explanation. I had several of these experiences that were stronger than usual that I would like to share to illustrate the goodness of God's protection and love.

I didn't often have to work late; my hours were pretty standard 8:30 a.m. to 4:30 p.m. One night, however, I was late at work and it was well past nine o'clock before I was ready to leave to go home. It wasn't the first night that I had ever worked late, although it was rare. This particular night as I started to leave the building to go to the parking lot, I saw it was dark outside and I felt this heavy cloak of fear all around me. I have always considered myself a strong woman, not one prone to unnecessary fear and certainly at this point in my life, not afraid of the dark. I attempted to wave off the uneasiness, but before I could take more than a few steps outside, the fear became palpable. I returned to the building and went to our Security office to request a "walk safe" guard, someone to accompany me to my car in the parking lot.

I had never requested this service before and felt a little silly doing so but the young security guard who escorted me out toward the parking lot, told me lots of people use the service and that was the reason he was there - to help me.

Even with the guard, I couldn't shake the feeling. The campus like many, although well-lit, is self-contained and isolated within itself and as we walked and got closer to the parking lot, I saw a car slowly driving up the long laneway toward us. In the car were two men who looked out of place and suspicious. I could see them conversing, and they stopped their car as they reached the crosswalk to the parking lot, to allow the guard and I to enter the parking lot by walking in front of the car. Once the guard and I passed by them, and we entered the parking lot, they slowly continued driving around the perimeter of the parking lot.

My heart was racing as I got into my car. I was even scared for the guard, so I sat in my car and watched as he returned to the campus entrance. I watched as the slow-moving car made several loops of the parking lot perimeter, before slowly driving out the way they had come. I waited a few moments and left for home, thankfully using a different exit than the car had because I was going the other way home.

Instinctively I gave thanks for God's mercy. I knew in my spirit that, had I come out alone, I would have encountered only God knows what at the hands of these two men; a much different outcome than the Good Samaritan intervention I had experienced many years previously, in Maine.

Another specific instance was some time much later. I had been shopping and I stepped out of the store onto the sidewalk, heading to the parking lot to my car. For no discernable reason, I had this immediate feeling to stop and look behind me as though I had dropped something when, in fact I knew I hadn't dropped anything. As strange as it seems I did stop, turn and look back. This only took a second. When I turned back to continue to my car, just as I was about to step off the sidewalk, a car sped past me at a very fast pace. I was shocked! Had I not taken that moment of delay, my next step would have taken me directly in the path of the speeding car.

Countless times I have been protected and saved by His heavenly promptings, interventions and beings. I am forever thankful and blessed that the Father sends His Spirit and His angels to light my path and guide my steps, not only when I least expect it but when I am not even *aware* of the danger ahead of me.

Take Off Your Shoes

The Lord God is my strength; He will make my feet like deer's *feet*, And He will make me walk on my high hills. - Habukkuk 3:19

God in His infinite mercy has chosen people to intervene in others' distress to help them in their times of need. My pleasure has been, as you have already learned, that on occasion He employs me in His desire to do so, just as He employs others to assist and guide me.

One November day, we got an unexpected early dumping of snow. The day had started out bright but brisk, as November days will be, but by midday it was evident that this storm was not just going to bring a dusting but a significant snow fall. I had left home that day for work with a coat but no boots, wearing my high heels as would normally be okay for this time of year.

I usually drive on the 401 Highway to go home but with this unexpected snowfall, I decided to take what I thought would be a less travelled, alternate route along Kingston Road to make better time and not get caught up in traffic. I was wrong; it seemed everyone had the same idea that I did. The traffic was inching along and I knew I would not get home for some time.

I got about two thirds of the way home and as I crested a hill, I saw drivers detouring around a disabled car, causing the two lanes to merge into one to get around, making even more of a mess in the traffic. I thought, *What an awful place to get stuck?* As I passed by the car, I saw a young lady sitting in the driver's seat. No one was with her, and all the cars just passed by her to get on their way in the snow storm. Her car hazard lights were on, but she looked rather desolate as I drove by. The traffic was getting worse as the snow continued to fall. I thought that this young lady needed help, and surely someone would stop and help her, and I kept on going.

Slowly, in the deepening snow, I inched further up the street, and then I heard the prompting. *Go back and help her.* I thought, *No* - I didn't want to go back. What could I do? I didn't know anything about cars, it was starting to get dark and the snow was not letting up. I found many excuses to continue along my way. I just wanted to go home. The Holy Spirit persisted, *Turn around and go back and help her.* I asked, *Why me?* but knew I had to turn around. About a half a block further along I found a service station driveway that I could drive into and turn my car around and did so.

When I got back to her car, I saw she was still alone; no one had stopped to help. The traffic was backed up in both directions and the only place I could park was in a street that intersected where her car had broken down. I put on my indicator so I could turn into the street only to find it was a very steep grade, but there was no place else to go. I drove onto the street and slowly turned my car around so my car would be facing down the hill and I could see her car. I was about eight car lengths away from her. Now what to do? I sat in my car and pondered my next move because I was parked on a steep hill, the snow was up past my ankles, and I had high heels on. There was no easy way down to her car.

As I sat pondering my dilemma, I again heard the prompting of the Holy Spirit, *Take off your shoes.* What was I hearing? There had to be at least three inches of snow on the ground and I only had pantyhose on in my heels. Surely, I wasn't being asked to go out in the show in my stocking feet, or so I thought. Then again clear as a bell, I heard, *Take off your shoes.* I knew arguing was futile, so I took off my shoes and reluctantly opened my car door. I stepped out and was concerned, not only because of the cold and wet snow, but also about the very steep hill. I was afraid I would slip and fall. I chose my steps very carefully as I inched down the hill toward her car. When I got to her, she opened the passenger-side door and I stepped in.

She was distraught. She had called her husband but they only had the one car and he was unable to come get her. He had called for a tow truck but they could not guarantee when they would get there with all the snow and accidents, and she had been sitting there for well over an hour already. She was cold and didn't know how much longer she would have to wait. I told her not to worry, that God was looking out for her. I told her how I had driven by and He made me come back to help her. She reacted as though she didn't believe me. She told me that "People don't do that. People just don't go out of their way to help." It was as though she had little faith in her personal life circumstance. I replied "But I did!," to reinforce the goodness that can abound when you have God in your life.

Since her husband had already called the tow truck, there was really nothing to do but wait. I assured her I would stay with her until her help arrived. I offered for her to come sit in my car where it was warm, and we walked together back to my car, in the cold through the snow. It wasn't until we got back in my car that she realized that I had no shoes on and she asked me why. I laughed and said I didn't know how I would walk down the hill in my heels so God told me to take off my shoes.

She did not comprehend what I was saying to her, this was so out of her realm of understanding. I repeated that God must really love her to make me turn around, come back in the storm, walk down the hill in my stocking feet in the snow to check on her.

I believe, if memory serves me correctly, that she said her name was Jackie. She called her husband when she got in my car and told him I had stopped and helped and was going to wait with her for the tow truck. He was relieved that she would not be waiting alone. As we talked, I got the overall sense that she and her husband were a close young couple experiencing some struggles, although she didn't share any details.

The tow truck eventually came. I stayed in my car while she went to talk with them. After she had spoken with them, she gave me a wave to let me know she was fine, and once I knew she was in good hands I left to continue on my way home.

I believe God had a purpose that night; He wanted Jackie and her husband to understand that He was present in their lives and their situation. Maybe it was in regard to the struggles they were facing or to renew her faith in humanity - I do not know. I just know that, once more, God had blessed me in a special way by meeting Jackie and having an opportunity to speak of His goodness and how He had intervened on her behalf this stormy evening.

When you listen and act on the prompting of the Holy Spirit there are blessings that will abound in many marvelous and often unexpected ways.

CHAPTER 5

Michael's Premonition

And as it is appointed for men to die once, but after this the judgement. - Hebrews 9:27

In the spring of 2007, Michael had taken his dad's new car to go to work one early Saturday morning. The roads were slippery as we had a late season snow, and Michael had gone off the road and hit a tree not too far from home. He called home and his dad and I took my car to the accident scene. By the time we got there, the police were on the scene and confirmed the accident was due to the weather and black ice; Michael was not at fault. Ed's car was in bad shape. More importantly, Michael was not hurt. Although the new car was, in fact, totaled Michael did not have a scratch. The accident could have had a terrible outcome but our boy was okay. We were so thankful to God for sparing our son any harm that day.

Later that year in early July 2007, I was driving Michael and I home from work at the college. We had been talking earlier in the ride, and he casually mentioned he needed some money. I didn't think anything of it because Michael had champagne tastes, he liked to dress well and invest in his shoe collection. He was also passionate about and working with his music, and studio time cost money. I didn't ask him what he needed the money for but I told him I could help him out with about two thousand dollars, he just had to let me know. He did not respond that he wanted any money from me so I just left it with him to consider.

We continued on the drive, and as we got closer to home Michael became unusually quiet. Out of the blue he said to me "Mom, people don't care when you die, they just go on with their lives." He was looking out the car window and added, "Look. Everyone is just going on about their business and people die every day. They just forget about you." Michael and I talked a lot about many things, and I said to him "Michael, when you die you are remembered and known by the love you leave behind. The people that love you, don't forget you." He seemed to think about that for a moment then before I could respond further, he asked me "Mom does it hurt when you die?" I was surprised by his question but answered the best I could and told him, "It depends on how you die." I told him "Even if someone was in pain such as in an accident or disease, then the minute they die, the pain is gone." I said something like, "I expect when death is upon you and you are in pain or are fearful, it lasts only up until the moment you pass into God's kingdom. Once you cross over, there you will rejoice and no longer remember your pain or fear."

In my mind this conversation was not strange as Michael and I talked so often about so many things. I was always proud that he would talk to me about anything, and I once overheard him tell his sister Sarah that she could talk to me about anything and trust I would be honest with her and answer any questions she had. So, this conversation did not raise any issues in my mind at the time. I went on to say in jest, "When the time comes, just remember to go toward the light." I said this to lighten the mood, but it was the truth nonetheless.

We had reached home by this point and the conversation ended, but this was just the beginning of what was to come of our family tragedy. I wish I had known what was in store for us. I wonder if the Heavenly Father was reaching out to Michael and I before our family tragedy. Was there any way to have averted what was to come?

My Beloved Michael Murdered

'Vengeance is Mine, and recompense; Their foot shall slip in *due* time; For the day of their calamity *is* at hand, And the things come to hasten upon them.' - Deuteronomy 32:35

Michael, our beautiful son, was shot on July 29, 2007 at 3:27 a.m. I know the precise time because that is the time the clock in his room stopped.

I had been uncharacteristically blissfully sleeping that night, when many nights I did not sleep well. Michael and I had an agreement that if he wasn't going to be home by 3:00 a.m., he had to call me so I knew he was okay and let me know what time he expected to get home. He was getting older, and at twenty-five, was exercising his independence, and I trusted him. I was almost always aware when Michael was not home, but because he had started to stay over, more regularly, at his girlfriend's house, I was getting more accustomed to him not being at home by the aforementioned 3:00 a.m.

The phone rang about 3:35 a.m. It was the call that every parent dreads. The call was an intense female voice screaming on the other end of the line. I was confused being awoken from a deep sleep and by the caller referring to me as "Mom" because I knew my daughter Sarah was in her bedroom down the hall. As the fog in my mind cleared, I realized it was Michael's girlfriend, Chanel and she was screaming into the phone "Mom! Mom! Michael is hurt! He has been shot and he isn't moving!" I realized my worst fears and became instantly awake. I asked where she was and she said she was at home. I said we'd be right there and hung up. By then Ed had awoken and Sarah had come to our bedroom door and I told them Michael has been hurt and we had to go to Chanel's. Sarah asked could she come with us and I told her she *had to* come with us. In my heart of hearts, I knew the worst.

Michael, as usual, had taken his dad's car when he went out

earlier that day, so I drove. When we got on to the highway, Ed asked, "What happened?", and I said just as Chanel had, "Michael's hurt, he's been shot and he is not moving." Ed and Sarah screamed simultaneously. They bombarded me with questions, but I did not have any answers, I told them that was all Chanel had said. I told them they needed to be strong because the situation was serious and I needed them to be ready for whatever was to come.

We got to the housing development where Chanel lived. There were many people standing around with Chanel and her brother Sheldon. We couldn't get farther down in the complex where her apartment was. Police tape was strung across the road and an ambulance and police car sat in front of her apartment building. A detective immediately came up to Ed, Sarah, and I and told us Michael had been shot and the paramedics were working on him. I asked could I go to the ambulance to see him and the detective told me to let the paramedics do their work because they were working hard to revive him. Time seemed to stop.

We spoke to Chanel and Sheldon and they had nothing to offer in the way of what happened. They said they had been inside and heard Michael's car pull up to the house. He had earlier gone to a party and was returning home to Chanel's. Then they heard the shots. Sheldon said they ran outside, and he was trying to speak to Michael and kept calling his name. He said Michael didn't speak but his fingers moved when Sheldon called out his name. They called 9-1-1; apparently so did a number of neighbours who heard the shots. Chanel said that is when she called me.

Waiting… waiting… waiting, and while watching the ambulance, I saw a faint wisp of light leaving the ambulance into the sky and it appeared to hover there. I didn't want to believe what I knew I was seeing. I knew Michael died in that moment I was watching. Moments later the lights in the ambulance all went dark. I simply said to no one in particular, "That's not good."

Minutes passed, and the detective approached us, coming from the ambulance and said "I guess you realize he didn't make it." I said, "I know, I saw him leaving." I became eerily calm and asked if I could now go see Michael. The detective said to me "Your son would not want your last memory of him to be to see him in the state he is in the ambulance." In that moment, I too felt Michael, always protective of me, would not have wanted me to see him like that, and I didn't go to the ambulance. I regret that I didn't go and hug him when I first arrived and the paramedics were trying to save his life, or after when their attempts were in vain. I wish I had gone to hug my boy one last time.

Sarah was standing beside me and jumped at the detective in anger and fear. I gently peeled her off him, and she turned to me and said, "Mommy we are lucky." I turned to her and incredulously said "Lucky?" and she said "Yes, we were blessed, we had Michael for twenty-five years." At that moment I knew an angel spoke through her because Sarah was only nineteen, she didn't "have" Michael for twenty-five years. It is this conversation that has been ingrained into my spirit and my heart. From that moment, I chose not to look at what I had lost, but to look at the awesome gift I had been given – twenty-five years of being Michael's mother. *Thank You Jesus.*

Even now, many ask me how I can function, how can I not hate, how can I face every day? This especially by those who knew the special bond Michael and I shared. I tell them and I tell you that I truly had been blessed by having my son for twenty-five years, that God is covering my heart and without Him I could not stand. God later shared the glory of the bond that Michael and I shared and I will share that with you further on.

After Sarah told me how blessed we were, I walked away by myself down the street of the complex and cried. Ironically and heartbreakingly, Michael was shot in the old neighbourhood community, three blocks from where we last lived when we started to hear gunshots at night and made the decision to purchase our home to protect our children from that negative atmosphere. As parents, Ed and I did all in we could in our power to keep our children safe. We moved; we made sure they were engaged in school; and our children were well adjusted, well liked, respectful and respected. It was to no avail. Our son was dead.

I eventually walked back to the crowd and we were all standing around in shock when Sarah began to speak as though she was speaking for Michael. She told Chanel that Michael was saying how he loved her and Sheldon. A butterfly came and landed on the front of Chanel's jacket. It wouldn't fly away even with Chanel's attempts to shake it off. I became concerned for Sarah because she continued to talk as though she were Michael; I told her it was too much for her and it was time to leave. I was becoming increasing concerned for her because those around were asking her questions and engaging in this dialogue.

Ed offered for Chanel and her brother Sheldon to come stay at our house because they could not go back to Chanel's apartment. Chanel and Sheldon stayed with us for some months and eventually made their separate ways to continue to try to live their lives the best way forward for them.

The detective had stayed in the background for a while to give us some privacy but eventually came up to tell us that we could go to the hospital to identify Michael's body and to see him. In a daze, we rode to the hospital only to find once we got there that he had given us incorrect information. As it turned out, when someone is already deceased, they do not take them to the hospital but directly to the morgue. The hospital staff was very confused as to why we had been sent there. We were sent home with a contact phone number for the morgue and we were told someone would call us to tell us when and where we could go to identify Michael's body.

It was hours later when Ed finally got in contact with someone who could tell us where Michael's body was. Sarah, distraught, went to her best friend Ahilia's house for comfort. I am forever grateful to Ahilia's family for embracing Sarah when she so desperately needed their love and care. Ed, Chanel and I left for the morgue. Once there we were led to a small room. We had to view Michael's body through a small window. We were unable to touch him or hug him because they had to do an autopsy. We were only permitted to look at him through the cold glass.

There was my precious beautiful boy, lying on this table, lifeless and cold. It was so very surreal to see Michael like this. He had been so full of life, love and especially laughter. Ed was the one who had the heart-breaking task to have to officially identify Michael, our son's, body. Our loss of Michael has taken an unmeasurable toll on us as a family, but Ed especially has never recovered sufficiently to be truly happy after the loss of his son.

Grand Foyer Revisited

For your Father knows the things you have need of before you ask Him. - Matthew 6:8

After we had spent some time viewing Michael's body through the glass, if memory serves me, we were taken across a narrow street and led into a building through a side door to wait for Ed to sign the identification papers. When we were let into the side door, it was darkened and it took some time to focus and to realize where we were. We were once again in the Grand Foyer of the Toronto Police Headquarters on College Street - the same grand room where I had received my Community Award just three years earlier!

When I look back on those commemorative pictures of the earlier celebration when I received my Toronto Police Service Award, which gave me such pride standing with my family, I think *Who would ever have thought that I would be back in that room and Michael would no longer be with me, with us?* I choose to take hold of my blessing that I have that glorious memory of the happiness of that earlier celebration and I was not left to solely experience the imposing starkness of death I now associated with the Grand Foyer. My Michael stooping to kiss me during the celebration, is the memory I choose to hold on to. *There are no coincidences in Christ.*

When Michael was shot to death I wondered of my Lord, *Why then? Why in such a horrific way and at the deliberate hand of someone?* I thought, *Lord, if You had to take my boy, why didn't You take him in the spring when he had the car accident in the snow.* It seemed that the pain of losing him in a car accident, would be easier to bear than having my boy shot, ambushed in a callous, cowardly, murderous act.

The Holy Spirit, as time went on, later revealed to me *why* Michael was taken in that way, although, not yet. At this time, to calm and comfort my heart and spirit God showed me His blessing and loving-kindness in that Michael had four additional months of life, love and laughter and I had him in my life for an additional four months. My spirit tells me that should be more than sufficient reason.

Thank You merciful Father for the extended time with my boy.

Wall of Angels

For He shall give His angels charge over you, To keep you in all your ways. - Psalm 91:11

In the days leading up to Michael's funeral, the house was filled with many friends and family providing support and comfort to Ed, Sarah and I. On this day we were mostly congregated in the kitchen adjacent to the dining room. Needing a break, I stepped into the dining room alone and started adjusting some of Michael's high school medals on the wall.

What happened next, happened in the twinkling of an eye. As I was adjusting the medals, I suddenly heard a loud sound of flapping wings. I thought a bird must have somehow flown into the house. I quickly turned towards the kitchen wondering who else heard it. In the moment I turned toward the kitchen, I miraculously saw the wall full of exquisite angels adorned in radiant white. They were suspended, as if on steps, one row above the other, covering the entire dining room wall. There were so many angels crowded together, one of the angels, which appeared to be smaller than the rest, had lost his footing. That was the sound I heard – the small angel's wings flapping as he attempted to catch his balance. Although I was stunned by what I had just witnessed, there was no reaction from any of my guests in the kitchen indicating that they had witnessed what I just did.

God, in that flash of a second in time, let me actually visually see the multitude of angels He had sent to watch out for me and our family at this tragic time. I knew He lifted His veil and gifted me with a miracle of supernatural sight so I could witness His hedge of protection and love. I had seen the glory of the Lord's compassion! From that instant I knew I had never, nor will ever, be alone and Michael was not alone at his passing or beyond.

I speak with authority to let you know He sends His angels to have charge over us. My first experience was when they lifted me up when I was home in Saint John for my sister Paula's funeral and they lifted me up and kept me from falling headlong down the stairs. Now I was blessed with the miracle of witnessing and seeing His angels in all their glory with my own eyes.

Thank You blessed Father for showing me Your majesty, through this wonderous sight.

Saying Goodbye

He who dwells in the secret place of the Most High shall abide under the shadow of the Almighty. I will say of the Lord, "*He is* my refuge and my fortress; My God, in Him I will trust." - Psalm 91:1-2

The day soon came that we were able to go to the funeral parlour to see Michael for the first time since he died; his body had been held at the morgue for several days to complete the autopsy. Ed, Chanel and I were there at the funeral home to bear witness to Michael's death. I was anxious about how I was going to react. I believe we were all fearful; this was a first for any of us to lose a close member of our family and one so dear to our hearts. I believe everyone was scared for me particularly, because Michael and I were so close. The funeral director took us to the waiting room and suggested that I go in to the chapel alone first. He said he would come with me and took me by the hand to lead me into the parlour where Michael lay.

When he opened the door, I could see Michael lying in repose at the far end of the room. I instinctively started to run toward my son still holding on to the funeral director's hand. He was hard-pressed to keep up behind me. I could not wait to get close to Michael and touch his face and tell him I loved him. He was so beautiful, even in death. Ed and Chanel gave me a few moments alone with Michael and then they came in as well.

Even though the funeral home staff were sensitive and caring, Ed and I sadly, and quickly had to come to learn about the business side of death. While in the throes of losing Michael, we had to choose his casket, work out all the funeral arrangements, and manage all the various payments. We had yet to find and book a church because at this time we did not have a church we were attending, find a Pentecostal pastor, decide and find what Michael was going to wear. Big things, small things - there were so many things to had to be done.

My heart broke that, in Michael's death, we had to put our feelings, our grief aside to organize, plan and make these difficult choices. His cousin Teesha who loved Michael so dearly offered to braid his hair to cover the bullet wounds, and in her grief, she had to put her feelings aside to ensure Michael was made presentable. The day we returned to the funeral parlour to deliver Michael's clothes and for Teesha to do his hair, it was all very peaceful and serene but

I recall the sad sight of my sister Karen sitting off and alone in her own grief and not coming close to Michael as he lay there.

My older brother Vaughn, from Dartmouth, Nova Scotia, called me before the funeral. Our conversation was short but direct. He wanted to ensure I still loved Christ. I told him, "Yes, I did." Losing Michael had not changed my love for Christ. I told him I understood God was no respecter of persons, but I always felt, in my heart, that I was special and even now, I remained faithful. God has a way of making all His children feel special.

Without a home church, we were at a loss for an officiating minister and relied on my friend Sandra to recommend a pastor who would perform Michael's funeral. Pastor Cataudella, a revered woman of God, readily agreed to perform Michael's funeral dedication service. We also found a church close to our home, Westney Heights Baptist Church, gracious in allowing us to host his funeral within their premises.

Ed allowed me to make the decision to have a closed casket for the visitation and funeral even though we prepared Michael for viewing. My reason seemed crystal clear to me at the time, I did not want whoever it was who shot him to have the opportunity or satisfaction to look at his dead body. We did not and still do not know who had done this and it hurt to think they could come and see him laid out in death. Having a closed casket is a decision I came to regret. In hindsight, by having Michael's casket closed, during the visitation at the funeral home as well as at the church funeral service, I took away the opportunity for his many friends and those who loved him their chance to say goodbye to him as they knew him. We had pictures of Michael all around and near the casket but it was not like seeing him and saying goodbye to the young man they knew. I am so sorry to Michael, and all his friends that I deprived of that closure in his passing.

The funeral was standing room only; the overfill room was filled and people spilled into the parking lot. Michael had so many who loved him. We also had so many out-of-town family and friends come to support us and pay their final respects. There was a multitude of current co-workers and associates, former co-workers of mine who had moved away and returned for Michael's funeral, some colleagues who drove, as a group, from Northern Ontario. Ed's co-workers and friends and a multitude of Sarah's friends, not only those who knew Michael, but knew him through each of us. We were so blessed in the outpouring of love shown to us that we decided to meet and greet everyone before the service rather than after.

To add a bit of levity to this utterly tragic story, I will share that during the meeting and greeting session, one of my work associates whom I didn't know well and whose first language is not English, came up to me crying, as were so many that day. As she hugged me, I believe she meant to whisper "Condolences," but thought I heard her whisper "Congratulations." Well, in the moment, I started to smile. My emotions were obviously not under my control. The next person in line must have thought I had lost my mind or was in shock, because I was suppressing a smile in the moment as I greeted her, just moments before the funeral. I never had an opportunity to explain so, if you are reading this book and you were that person, now you know why I was trying so hard not to smile before the funeral of my beloved son.

Before the service began, the family, as is normal practice, was invited in to the chapel and seated before the guests. After we were seated, as the guests filed in to the chapel sanctuary, we heard Michael's voice over the chapel speakers. Ed had arranged with the church to play a song that Michael had written for me several years before, "I Love You Mama." Many guests were brought to tears, and there were numerous gasps as we all heard Michael's words being broadcast in his recorded love song to me. I am forever grateful to Ed for orchestrating this to happen for all of us in attendance and to Michael for his gift of recorded love to me. I will share the background and his love song, shortly.

Michael's uncle Kevin performed the eulogy, Michael's aunt Karen and cousin Teesha offered scripture readings, and a number of Michael's friends gave tributes of him. Chantal wrote and recited a heart-felt poem dedicated to her brother. She lovingly referred to Michael as "Blue" because that was by far his favourite colour. His older sister Chantal Levesque is my oldest daughter born before marriage. She united with us and was strongly embraced in our family late in Michael's childhood and was devoted to us as we were to her. It broke my heart that she and Sarah had to say goodbye to their only brother.

Near the end of the service, before Pastor Cataudella performed Michael's Benediction, she silently motioned to me an invitation, as we had pre-arranged, for the opportunity to speak, as I wasn't sure I would be up to it until the moment came. But God, in His infinite mercy, gave me strength when I saw the overwhelming outpouring of love, and I just had to publicly say goodbye to our boy and express our family's appreciation for everyone's support. Michael had touched everyone in that room in a significant way. By the grace of God, I was able to stand strong and proud, to offer everyone in attendance encouragement and love in return, to soften their grief.

I Love You Mama

Love suffers long *and* is kind; love does not envy; love does not parade itself, is not puffed up; does not behave rudely, does not seek its own, is not provoked, thinks no evil; does not rejoice in iniquity, but rejoices in the truth; bears all things, believes all things, hopes all things, endures all things. - 1 Corinthians 13:4-7

I need to go back a number of summers before the funeral when Michael had asked me to put a relaxer in his hair. He didn't want to go to a hairdresser to have it done and trusted only me to relax his hair, just as he only trusted his cousin Teesha to braid it. His hair was his crowning glory. It had grown past his shoulders and he liked to have it straight. This day was a sunny Saturday afternoon and we were sitting in the kitchen. Just as I was ready to begin to apply the relaxer, he asked me to hold on and wait a moment he had to go upstairs. I was impatient because I was just about to start the process and quite frankly, I wanted to get it done, because I had a few errands I wanted to run that day. I often tried to get Michael to make an appointment to get his hair professionally relaxed but he insisted that I do this for him.

Michael came back downstairs with his CD player and he put a CD in and told me to listen to the song. He often had new music to listen to so this was no different until I heard the words of the song. He had written a song for me called, "I Love you Mama." My heart burst with love and pride that he took the time to write his feelings and thoughts and put them into this song dedicated to me. The song was heartfelt and personal, from him to me. I hugged him and told him I loved him, how beautiful the song was, and how proud I was of him, trying not to let him see me cry. Michael was so proud and happy that he had given me this piece of joy from his heart and he was pleased I was obviously overwhelmed with it.

This gift of his love song is my forever living link to my boy. Since Michael died, whenever I feel lonely or miss him or just want to feel near to him, I can listen to his voice through his song, and remember his love for me.

I am often reminded of the now unsettling conversation Michael and I had on our drive home from work in the weeks preceding his demise, speaking about death and dying. Now that he is no longer with me, his song is equally haunting. Nothing makes me happier than to share the beautiful lyrics of his song with you here, so you can judge for yourself. (Spoken and written in hip-hop vernacular.)

I Love You Mama

Aha Aha

To the one who always had my back
To the one I don't ever think I can pay back
When I look into your face, I see me looking back
The only female that I know deserve her own track
I love you mama

Please believe me and this song will tell ya
That you one of the few reasons why I ain't a failure
Because you stand behind me, all my thoughts, wishes, dreams
And do the best to help me accomplish them by any means.
I know it seems that I'm doing nothin' every day,
And you when ask me something real all I do is play
But honestly every day all I do is pray
To finally make it and to carry you before you lay
That's real talk and in your eyes, I can do no wrong
Respect your wishes only time I cuss is in my songs
And when I feel like letting go you force me to hold on
To the number one woman that's in my life,
Scherry George my mom - that's my mom

You told me it was cool to cry
The day I told you I don't want to live to see you die
It really hurt you when I stood back and thought why
You'd help me bake it, but not really care to eat my pie
I'm so proud when I see so much of you in me – yup
And the person that you helped mold me to be

You told me, "Michael, blaze your tree but responsibly"
You're like an angel watching over me – constantly.
I ought to be outside somewhere doing crimes, and selling lines
But instead, I'm writing rhymes with matching lines
And during hard times I'd never know
Was always eating, always clothed, man it never showed
And when I was going nowhere fast you would help me slow
And now I growed into the man I thought I'd never know
And there's only so many ways I can say thanks
But thank God every day that I have the chance
"Thank You."

Aha Aha

In 2009, to honour Michael and Michael's love for me through this song, Ed worked with some of Michael's music-studio friends and found a way that Sarah and I could record an extension on Michael's CD. Here are our words added to Michael's on the CD.

Sarah:

Mommy we're so lucky – We had Michael for 25 years!

Me:

Michael, those words which were spoken through an angel that eve,
Was God's grace undeniable so my heart wouldn't grieve.
Those words are my comfort, those words are my joy.

God could choose anyone, but let you be my boy.
I've been so blessed in your love left behind,
Cherishing sweet memories, each new treasure to find.
So, son rest in peace until that glorious day
Jesus brings us together, forever to stay.
"I love you Michael."

As you can probably understand or imagine, this CD is precious to me on so many levels. Every opportunity I have, I give it to those I feel will appreciate the love that Michael and I shared, and it has poignantly touched the hearts of all who have been fortunate enough to be gifted with Michael's, "I Love You Mama" CD.

We decided Michael was going to be cremated. Well, it was my idea but Ed was so compassionate toward my feelings he allowed me to make that final decision because I could not bear to put my boy in the ground. I wanted to hold on to Michael as long as I could and, in a sense, I felt I could accomplish this by keeping his remains in a commemorative urn as long as I wanted to. I also wanted to feel a part of me would be with him forever, so the day before the funeral I cut a lock of my hair, and asked the funeral parlour cosmetician to promise to place it in Michael's breast pocket before he was cremated. After the funeral service the cosmetician told me he had done so, that my hair was safely tucked in Michael's breast pocket as they prepared to take him to the crematorium. I was thankful that a part of me would be with him forever.

Baby Consoler

Blessed are those who mourn, For they shall be comforted. - Matthew 5:4

Earlier on I told you I would share an experience of a poignant example of a baby's discernment, and now I shall. The day of

Michael's funeral, after the service, many people came back to our house and some of us were in the kitchen. Many other family members and friends were outside on the back deck and in the yard. One of our family friends Basil, recently remarried, and had a new son with his wife. Basil had an older son who was a friend of Michael's, and our families had known each other since before the older boys were born. Some of us stood talking in the kitchen and congratulating the couple on the new child, when Basil's wife held out the baby for me to hold. I was reluctant to hold this child since I had just come from the funeral service for Michael, but a number of people were there looking on and I felt obliged to do so. I took the baby in my arms and collectively everyone gasped, myself included.

This tiny newborn baby looked directly in my eyes, put his little hand on my heart and laid his head on my chest. It was a moment stopped in time, and everyone knew this was a moment they would not - could not - ignore or forget. I was shaken by this experience at the time, it startled me. To this day I regret that I did not embrace the baby and relish the moment. I mumbled something like, *"this is too strange,"* and handed the baby back to his mother.

What knowledge this child may have possessed as a witness to my grief? I squandered a cherished moment with which the Lord had wanted to bless me.

"Forgive me Father God for not recognizing and accepting Your gift of compassion and consolation offered to me through this newborn child."

Michael Visits Sarah

Let brotherly love continue. - Hebrews 13:1

After Michael died, a number of unexplained events happened in our home in addition to those shared already. A few weeks or so after Michael's funeral service the house was quiet. There was no one home but Sarah and I. There were no guests and Ed had returned to work.

Sarah was quietly lying on the couch in the family room and I went in to see if she needed anything or wanted to talk. I was utterly astonished to see an image of Michael's spirit hovering about four inches above her body, laid out as if he was prone on top of her. I clearly could see Sarah through Michael's spirit, which was transparent and suspended just above her. I noticed that Michael's long hair was gone; his hair was short and cropped close to his head. I stopped in my tracks dumbfounded! The vision did not disappear. Time seemed to stop and after a few moments Sarah turned to me and asked me what was wrong. Michael's image vanished. She had not seen Michael's spirit; she simply saw me walk into the room and fixate my gaze on her. How could I tell her I saw Michael's spirit keeping company with her? I stammered that I thought she was sleeping and I had come in to turn off the television she was watching. I told her to go ahead and continue watching because I didn't realize she was awake.

I immediately left the family room, went upstairs to my bedroom and sat on the edge of the bed to collect my thoughts. I asked myself, *What did I just see?* I had to record in my own mind that I had in fact just seen Michael's spirit.

Although I have experienced many strange occurrences in my life, each time something happens I try to recognize and rationalize the situation to attest to my own beliefs and understanding. This was one such time.

Michael Listened In

Therefore if *there is* any consolation in Christ, if any comfort of love, if any fellowship of the Spirit, if any affection and mercy, fulfill my joy by being like-minded, having the same love, *being* of one accord, of one mind. - Philippians 2:1-2

I will be forever grateful to my neighbor Marie, who came to visit and sit with me first thing every morning for more than three weeks following Michael's funeral, to have a cup of tea and just to lend her motherly inspired love and support in my loss of Michael. Naturally, by this time, everyone else who had been visiting had returned to their day to day lives, making her comfort, caring and love more deeply and warmly welcomed.

Marie lives two houses from us and her son Graig was one of Michael's closest friends. Graig and Michael spent a lot of time in our respective homes growing and maturing as young men, and each were welcomed, unofficially, as adopted sons in each other's families.

Many of Michael's friends spent time at our home, especially in the summer, swimming in our pool and enjoying Ed's barbeque skills. Graig especially enjoyed and appreciated my popular macaroni pie. He was an ever-present addition and most welcome as he and Michael formed a strong brotherhood relationship since we had moved into the neighbourhood twelve years earlier. They forged a bond as many young men do who spend time together through their formative years, with school, girls, basketball and music; not necessarily in that order.

Graig was devastated when Michael was killed, as were many of Michael's friends. He often came over to visit and chat with me just to see how we were doing in the time after Michaels' death, offering his support and comfort. On one of these occasions early one evening, he and I were sitting in our living room, which Michael and Sarah had dubbed the "the white room" because we used it only for special occasions, prior to Michael's passing. We called it the white room as the furniture was all white and, like many families, when the kids were younger, they were not allowed to play in there. Graig and I were talking and reminiscing about Michael through telling stories and laughter; Michael's signature personality trait, with both of us trying to be strong for the other, trying not to break down.

In the midst of our conversation, I heard one of my ornamental snow globes on the coffee table between us briefly come on and play music. This was extraordinary because each of the several snow globes I had on the table, needed to be wound to play the music, and they had all lain dormant for quite some time. I did not see, nor did I discern any immediate reaction from Graig to acknowledge the sound of the music that played. So, I just continued on with the conversation in which Graig and I were engrossed.

A few moments later, the snow globe music played again, and this time Graig stopped what he was saying to ask me "Did you hear that?" to which I replied, "I heard it the first time." This was so unusual. Although I had had a number of strange things happen in the house, I had never before, simultaneously, shared any experience with another person.

Graig then acknowledged he too had heard the music the first time but thought he was imagining it. We agreed that the music had to be the result of Michael making his presence known, as we sat and conversed about him. What a complete feeling of astonishment and joy that he was there with us as we spoke. After we acknowledged Michael's presence by saying "Hi Michael," we both found ourselves fighting tears of sadness in our loss of my son, and his friend. A jumbled mix of emotions overwhelmed Graig and I; love, joy, wonder, surprise, happiness, sadness and longing.

It was amazing to share this experience with Graig, for both of us to know that Michael's spirit had not only visited with us and listened in on our conversation, but that he had found a way to let us know he was there with us.

Comforter or Comforted

Blessed *be* the God and Father of our Lord Jesus Christ, the Father of mercies and God of all comfort, who comforts us in all our tribulation, that we may be able to comfort those who are in any trouble, with the comfort with which we ourselves are comforted by God. - 2 Corinthians 1:3-4

I was generously given bereavement leave from the college for five weeks. More time was offered for me to process my grief, but Sarah was returning to the college for the fall 2007 semester of study, and I didn't want her to have to return alone. Memories of Michael were in the hallways since he graduated in 2005, after attending as a student for three years. After graduation he worked in Enrolment Services part-time until he was murdered in 2007. Michael had been at the college for a total of five years and his presence would be sorely missed. I chose to return to work so Sarah would feel more comfortable returning for her study. I couldn't let her return alone.

At the end of the first week back to work, I was getting ready for bed that Friday evening and I was emotionally drained. I had spent the week speaking with, crying with, and comforting people as Michael was well known and well loved. I was exhausted. Silently but vehemently, I cried out to the Lord, "Why am I being the person hugging others and making them feel better? I was Michael's mother! Shouldn't people be hugging me and comforting me?" I distinctly heard, *Do you want to be the comforter or the comforted?*

Instantaneously I understood the implications of my answer; and I understood God was asking me how I wanted to proceed from this moment. I understood that either I could choose to stand and be strong for others or others would have to hold me up in my grief. Since Michael died, I had many times imagined my shadow laid out beside me in grief, where I would *actually* be without Christ's mercy, grace and loving-kindness toward me. I knew if things were as they should be, I would be flat out, face down, inconsolable in my grief.

I chose to be, and remain, the comforter. *Thank You Father.*

Michael Visits His Dad

He heals the brokenhearted, And binds up their wounds. - Psalm 147:3

I could hardly contain my amusement after hearing Ed's story one day after I arrived home from work to find him standing outside on the front step. It was late October of the same year Michael had died and it was chilly outside, as the weather had begun to get colder. Ed was not in the habit of standing outside in the cold for no reason, so that was my first clue that something was amiss.

Whenever Ed got home from work before me, he started supper so when Sarah and I came home from work and school, supper would not be so late. This late afternoon when I pulled into the driveway, Ed met us on the front step and I could see he was very agitated.

He said that he had been in the house and Michael was "in there." He said he heard Michael running down the stairs from the second floor while running his hands down the wall. It totally unnerved Ed. He is not prone to believing anything he cannot see, touch, feel, taste, or hear. Many of the occurrences in this book are ones I have not previously shared, and many will come as a surprise to him. I learned early in our marriage that he is not a believer in the supernatural so I have kept quiet throughout the years concerning these things. But now, here he was, face to face with his own supernatural experience. It shook him to his core and was the basis of my amusement.

Michael had formed this particular habit over the years. Most times when he was on his way downstairs, he would run his hand down the wall on the way down. It made noise, not to mention the occasional fingerprint marks on the wall. He was always being told, "Michael, stop running your hand down the wall, it leaves marks," but it became a habit, and I'm not sure he actually tried to put an end to it.

So, this is how Michael manifested his presence and visited his dad when he was alone in the house, so his dad would know it was him. Ed said he heard the sound of Michael's hands dragging on the wall and as though he was running down the stairs. Ed was shaken and scared by this experience. I assured him it was Michael just making his presence known to him and there was nothing to be afraid of, that Michael would never do anything to harm him. I said if it ever happened again to simply acknowledge his presence by saying hello, because that is all Michael was attempting to do by his visit - say hello to his dad, his pal.

Lenny

Because You have been my help, Therefore in the shadow of Your wings I will rejoice. - Psalm 63:7

Sarah and I were returning home from the college some time after I had returned to work and Sarah returned to her fulltime study after our bereavement leave. As we pulled into the driveway, there sitting on the step, in front of our house was a young cat, bigger than a kitten but not full grown either. As we approached the house, the cat came directly toward me. It was cute, but I was reluctant to touch it or pick it up because I have a severe cat allergy. As I opened the front door, the cat brushed by us and promptly went inside, as though it lived there. I told Sarah to "Get the cat," due to my allergies, so Sarah caught up with and picked up the cat. It was so cute and playful, but I told Sarah to put it outside. I figured the cat would go home, surely someone must be looking for it; it was still just a kitten.

Sarah put the cat outside and she kept peeking through the glass to watch the cat, but it didn't leave the front step. She told me after a while that he was still outside, so I told her she could to take out some milk for him. Sarah gave the cat some milk and I went upstairs to change my clothes so I could start supper before Ed got home.

The cat faithfully returned for a number of days, sitting on the steps waiting for us when we came home. When we let it come inside, it would attempt to follow either Sarah or I, not leaving one or the other of us, and following one of us at every step. I was surprised through all this interaction with the cat, my allergies were not bothering me at all. After a few days of this, we figured the cat had adopted us. Sarah asked me if we could keep it, and I said we first had to determine if anyone had lost it and was looking for it.

In the meantime, Sarah and I went out to buy some cat food and some cat toys. We had been feeding it tuna, and I asked Sarah what she wanted to name him. "Lenny" she said. I wasn't surprised, Sarah named everything Lenny since she was a little girl. I told her we had to at least try to find the owner before we kept him. So, we set out in the car to a few of the neighbourhood pet stores to see if there were any postings of a lost cat. We eventually had exhausted checking all the shops but we didn't find any lost cat postings, and we happily decided Lenny now had a home with us, and we decided to keep him. He was the most affectionate cat I had ever interacted with. We had become as attached to him, as he certainly was attached to us.

Once we had done our due diligence of attempting to find his owner, satisfied we had not found anyone who had lost him, we felt comfortable in our decision to keep him. We next went to a neighbourhood veterinary office, intending to get him checked out and have the vet administer any shots he needed. As sour luck, yes *sour* luck, would have it when we got there, Sarah saw a "lost cat" sign. The picture was grainy and not very clear, but undeniably, it was Lenny. We didn't want to believe it was him, but it was, and it was heart-breaking for us.

We sadly came home and called the number posted under his picture. Yes, she had lost her cat. I explained how the cat was unusually clingy and loving. The owner confirmed that sounded like her pet and was so glad we found him. She told me she had recently moved out of the neighbourhood and temporarily left the cat with her mother until she got settled, but the cat had run away. She was anxious to get her cat back and made arrangements to come later that evening to pick him up. I tried to tell her the next day would be fine, wanting more time with Lenny before we had to give him up, but she was missing him and wanted him back as soon as possible.

She arrived at our home later that evening. With heavy hearts, Sarah and I sadly turned Lenny over to her with all his newly bought food and toys. Once Lenny was gone, Sarah shared with me that she felt the cat was embodied by Michael's spirit to come to visit us. I was not ready to accept her synopsis at the time, but upon later reflection, I realized that this situation was very bizarre. The cat had been so strangely attached to us, and especially notable, was that my severe allergies had not been activated! Even Ed, who is not a proponent of the supernatural, believed there was something extraordinary about this cat and it`s curious attachment to Sarah and I.

CHAPTER 6

God's Grace and Mercy

And the peace of God, which surpasses all understanding, will guard your hearts and minds through Christ Jesus. - Philippians 4:7

Ashamedly, I admit I was still not attending any church in 2007 when Michael died, although the Lord had been faithfully calling me long before this tragedy through His intended meeting of, and my subsequent relationship with, my co-worker Judy. God also attempted to have me return to Him through my best friend Sandra, who also had found Him as her personal Lord and Saviour. She also encouraged me to go to church with her and was met with my resistance and excuses. So therefore, through my own actions, I found when Michael died, I did not have a home church to lean on for support or comfort and thus had to rely on Sandra to recommend Pastor Cataudella for his funeral.

I found it necessary to rely once more on Pastor Cataudella's spiritual guidance in October 2007, and I went to her church to speak with her. Her church was not far from my office, so I went to see her on a lunch break and took a small offering for her church, knowing through Sandra that her church was experiencing financial constraints. I went for spiritual guidance because my heart was not feeling the depth of grief that I thought I should be experiencing based on the deep relationship Michael and I shared. I felt guilty that I was not laid out in grief and despair, that I was strong and comforting others in Michael's death. Even though I understood the implication of responding that I wanted to be the comforter rather than the comforted, my human nature felt guilty that I was not more distraught. Unfortunately, in Toronto and the surrounding areas many mothers, parents had lost their children, as tragically as I had lost Michael, through gun violence, but their expressions of grief appeared to be more heartfelt, and raw.

I shared with Paster Cataudella I thought something was wrong with me. My relationship with my son was, to me, stronger than any bond I could explain. So why wasn't I incapacitated and inconsolable like the other mothers who had lost their sons to horrific gun violence?

Pastor Cataudella explained to me God's grace, His unmerited favour, and told me that I should accept the peace in my heart because it was a gift, just like Michael had been. God loved me and through His mercy, I was being spared the overwhelming devastation of losing my precious son, through the grace of Christ Jesus. She could not explain why but said it is not for us to question; we just need to accept His blessing, His grace and His peace.

Based on this revelation, I asked her if I could come to her church the following Sunday and address her congregation and give thanks for the beautiful blessing that remained in my life, my daughter Sarah. She granted me that opportunity and I remember the congregation was surprised, but uplifted that, although I had recently lost my son, I could stand and give thanks for my daughter. Only God knows why I was prompted to stand and make this declaration of faith and love to her congregation, but it was important for me to stand and publicly declare His glory in the face of this devastating adversity.

Later, it will become clear why I was, and remain, so calm in the loss of my precious son as shared with me through the Holy Spirit.

Jenny's Healing

But He *was* wounded for our transgressions, *He was* bruised for our inequities; The chastisement for our peace *was* upon Him, And by His stripes we are healed. - Isaiah 53:5

As I left Pastor Cataudella's church after seeking her spiritual advice, I could feel the physical presence of the Holy Spirit on me as I returned to work. I had experienced the same sensation long before in my home town, praying and worshipping with my friend Toni, in our kitchen. Just as before, my peripherical vision was framed by sparkling light, and it was almost difficult to see to drive. I didn't quite realize it in that moment, but God had job for me which I was not expecting.

When I got back to the college, while immersed in this vision of light as I walked across the bridge entrance returning to the campus, I heard, *Pray for Jenny.* Jenny, a coworker, was diagnosed with thyroid cancer in February 2002. Jenny had worked side by side with Michael in the financial aid office at the Morningside campus and the two of them had forged a special relationship. Jenny was heartbroken when Michael was killed, and I have often said Jenny loved my Michael almost as much as I. She has a beautiful daughter and she also has a son, called "Mike" with an April birthday, just like my boy.

I was taken aback by the *Pray for Jenny* prompting. Not that I didn't want to pray for Jenny, but I was uncomfortable to ask her to pray. Although I felt had a personal relationship with God, I was not at this time attending a church or having any type of religious fellowships, and I certainly was not publicly praying for people, seemingly out of the blue. I tried to discount what I was hearing, but I heard again, *Pray for Jenny.* God was clearly telling me to pray for her.

When I got back inside the campus, I called her to my office and asked if I could pray for her. Until this time, we had never prayed together or talked together about God. Jenny appeared to be surprised that I had asked her to pray, and even more surprised when I told her God told me to. She accepted the prayer request, and we self-consciously prayed together that day, for the first time. I believe Jenny was healed of her cancer this day, which will become apparent later in the book. Many more opportunities arose over the years that Jenny and I and others would pray.

I'm Alright

Who remembered us in our lowly state, For His mercy *endures* forever. - Psalm 136:23

It is unfathomable how things work in the spiritual world, for which I can offer no explanation, but can only recall and share my experiences. Michael had a number of stuffed animals, mostly puppets, with which I would spend hours entertaining him and Sarah throughout their childhoods. Michael liked to collect and name these animals. His favourites were a small yellow bear named Cuddles; Yawny, a puppet whose mouth opened wide when you put your hand in to move him; and there was Joey, a little puppet fox. There were many other stuffed animals that he collected, ones that when you pressed their bellies, or their toes, they would make a particular sound. One example was a karate bear that made a "hi-karate" sound when you poked his belly, which Michael found quite hilarious.

As Michael got older, he was given stuffed animals and gifts by a number of young ladies suiting his fancy. He kept these things in his room. One quiet day after his passing, I was in his room just spending time remembering him with his girlfriend Chanel. We were sadly reminiscing about our lost love, and I noticed on his dresser a larger stuffed toy, not the cutest, I might add. At first, I thought it was a beaver, but upon inspection found there was no flat tail so I presumed it was a groundhog or a gopher. As I said, we were just hanging out feeling melancholy and then I noticed a button on the base of the groundhog and I pressed it. The groundhog began to move and sway in an animated dance and began to sing.

Chanel and I were thunderstruck that, just when we needed some comfort, here was this stuffed groundhog toy dancing and singing a song that let us know Michael was okay and in a good place and we needn't be worried about him. Unfortunately, copyright laws preclude my sharing the name of the song or the words with you at this time.

How could we not feel that God was reaching out to us at just the time when we needed to hear from Michael the most, letting us know he was okay and not to worry about him? He had been taken in such a sudden and horrific way, but this dancing and singing groundhog was a comfort and a blessing to our hearts and spirits. In our sadness, our gracious Lord touched us through a humourous antic that was so like Michael!

We serve an awesome God who understands the touch we need to ease our pain and grief when we need it the most and permits spiritual interventions to ease our suffering.

Baptized

And he arose and came to his father. But when he was still a great way off, his father saw him and had compassion, and ran and fell on his neck and kissed him. - Luke 15:20

God was patiently waiting for me. His arms were wide open to welcome me back into His loving embrace when I was ready to accept Him once more into my life, even though I had disregarded His reaching out to me for so many years. It took the loss of my precious Michael for me to heed the call of the Lord and reconnect with His teaching through the church. Remembering how the Lord had reached out to me over the years, I was saddened that I had told my co-worker Judy, as well as my friend Sandra, so many times that I would come back to the church "when the time was right." Well, here I was, now bended and bowed, seeking my Father for forgiveness and His embrace.

Sandra was glad to finally have me join her at the Agincourt Pentecostal Church (APC). There I found a sense of love and family, comfort and caring. In addition to Sunday services, I started to attend weekly Bible study lessons. I was never very good at retaining the scripture and teachings, the things I saw other Christians do. But God never let go of me. In all that time I was away from Him, He was never away from me. He accepted me now as I came with all my flaws and faults, ready to come to Him with a full heart of commitment. I sought to hear His voice, feel His comfort. I was searching to fill the void in my life that was so deep after losing Michael. I wanted to increase my understanding of God and to reconnect with the fellowship within the church through the Bible.

I was happy attending church, and through my Bible study leader, was invited to attend the APC satellite church, the Kingston Road Community Church (KRCC), where he served as pastor. This was a wonderful time of learning and becoming whole again, and God continued to show me His grace, glory and love for me. He continued to give me wondrous experiences, and when I spoke with the elders of the congregation, they marveled at what God was doing in my life. They expressed to me that "great things" happen to new Christians, as though I had not already had these experiences in the past. They didn't know my past and the many blessing that God had provided to me thus far. He had blessed me throughout my life and continued to bless me now. I was reminded in my spirit that I did have a relationship with Christ all along because He loved me and would never forsake me.

Ed, Sarah and Teesha also eventually started to regularly attend church and built their own relationships with Christ, accepting Him as their Lord and Saviour. Sarah, Teesha and I were baptized in April of 2008. My baptism opened a spiritual doorway that may not have otherwise opened, as the Lord continued to bless me in many ways and shape my inner being, making me want to be a better person and leading me to a higher spiritual awakening.

While at KRCC, I came to know and care for so many fellow Christians as they too genuinely cared for me and one another, I felt I was finally home. God has given me such amazing brothers and sisters in Christ that it is impossible to name them all here. I pray they know who they are and how much I cherish them in my spiritual growth. One sister in particular still provides me with unconditional love, a quiet but forceful woman, always willing to be a prayer partner in all areas of my life. Over the years I have come to rely on her as a true, steadfast friend as well as my confidante and big sister in Christ. My dear sweet sister Del (Deloris). I thank God for her every day.

Forgiveness of a Lie

And be kind to one another, tenderhearted, forgiving one another, even as God in Christ forgave you. - Ephesians 4:32

Earlier on I had shared with you how proud I was the day I overhead Michael tell his younger sister, Sarah, that she could trust me with anything or ask me anything and I would always be honest and truthful with her. I relished that memory at the time, but sometime later I spoke, and held onto a lie, with my family. My heart was wrenching because Michael had died before I had a chance to confess my lie to them. It was laying on my heart heavily since I had gotten baptized.

The summer before he died, I went to the hospital to visit a co-worker's mother. I went into her room and spoke with her and as a matter of greeting I patted her hand and kissed her cheek. I was quite fond of her and thought nothing of my actions. But when a nurse entered, although she did not have on any protective coverings, she became quite concerned to find me in the room and told me to go to the nurse's stations to get a covering or I would have to leave. I had entered the room without noticing a warning sign on the door advising visitors to go to the nurse's station before entering, so they could be given a protective covering. I am not sure what medical issue she was experiencing, but whatever it was must have been serious.

I decided to leave, I was only going to visit for a short time anyway, but all the way home I wondered if I had contracted something by being in her room and touching her. I was scared.

When I got home, during dinner I told the family about my visit and that I had missed the warning sign on the door that I should not have entered without protection. I tried to make light of it; after all the nurse who came into the room did not have on any protective gear. Ed asked me if I touched her. I lied. I said I had not touched her.

I carried this lie for a number of months before Michael died. I felt remorse for lying in the first place; that I could have put my family in jeopardy, did not own up to it and now Michael had died with this lie between us. I could never make it right with him.

One evening my conscience was suddenly and unexpectedly on fire. It had escalated to a frantic scream in my head. I just had to confess to Ed and Sarah that I had lied and I had to confess *right now*. I prayed to God for guidance in how I could tell them, asking Him to be with me in the telling. Notwithstanding Michael's tragic death and funeral, this was one of the hardest things I ever had to do. I expected them to be justifiably angry for potentially putting their health at risk, and I was fearful for the ramifications I thought would follow my confession. I felt I had let them down terribly, especially Sarah, since Michael had told her I would always be truthful. I deserved any reactions of anger and disappointment that would come my way; after all, not only had I put the family in potential harm's way, I then lied about it. How could I have done that?

I prayed again before facing the situation head-on. We were

all upstairs, and I said to Ed and Sarah that I wanted to speak with them. We weren't much for family meetings so both of them looked surprised. I told them I had something to tell them, I had a confession. They looked concerned and listened intently as I told them about the day when I visited my friend's mother in the hospital, that I had in fact touched her and I had kissed her on the cheek. I told them I was ashamed at what I had done and how sorry I was that I had put them in jeopardy and that I lied about it. I told them I was so sorry that Michael had died, and I didn't now have the chance to tell him what I had done. I was mortified making this confession.

What followed was immediate, totally unexpected and full of God – forgiveness! Neither of them expressed any anger toward me, neither did they look at me with the disappointment or disgust that I had been expecting. They exchanged looks before looking back at me and Ed said, "Okay then, to make up for it you have to take us out to dinner." Just like that it was over.

I was bewildered, shocked and beyond relieved that this lie I had harboured in my heart, along with the overwhelming remorse and guilt, was all washed away and immediately forgiven. Ed and Sarah had shown me grace in my confession. God was indeed by my side.

We went to dinner later that week at Swiss Chalet, and the issue was never spoken of again.

"Mommy, I've Been Murdered"

That the God of our Lord Jesus Christ, the Father of glory, may give you the spirit of wisdom and revelation in the knowledge of Him, the eyes of your understanding being enlightened. - Ephesians 1:17-18

God bound Michael and I together with cords of love that could not be broken. My daughters Sarah and Chantal are exquisitely loved; wholly and fully in my heart and my being, unconditionally.

But God had a special purpose for my and Michael's lives, and it was all made clear to me this night.

Some months after Michael died, I was sitting alone in the white room, just quietly missing him and reflecting on his life and our relationship. I was deep in thought when I heard a whisper, *Remember when*. I was quietly surprised and I heard it again, *Remember when*. I surrendered to the whisper and let my mind go. I heard, *Remember, when Michael was little and said to you "Mommy, I've been murdered!"* The memory came tumbling back into my consciousness.

When Michael was a little boy about three years old, one of his favourite activities was colouring. He and I spent a lot of time together on the floor or at the kitchen table colouring in one of his many books. This particular day I had taken him out to run a few errands, and during our travels we had picked up a new coloring book and some crayons. He proudly carried the bag containing his new items. As we continued on our errands at the next store we came to, Michael wanted to take the bag with his new book and crayons with him, but I told him no, we would leave them in the stroller, outside the store. I put the crayons and the colouring book on the small shelf under the seat of his stroller.

We finished that errand, and as we exited the store, Michael looked down on the shelf where we had left his precious purchases. Suddenly, he stood up and said, "Mommy, I've been murdered!" I felt an immediate stab in my heart and in my spirit for a couple of reasons. First, Michael was not old enough to be putting full sentences together and he certainly did not know the word *murdered*. I immediately corrected him and said "No, no, Michael, you have been robbed, the word is *robbed*." He stood up to his full height, looked right at me and firmly corrected me: "No, Mommy, I've been murdered." I was scared, he was adamant and sure of what he was telling me, and I knew he should not be aware of either word, *murdered* or *robbed*. He was far too young.

As the recollection now crystalized in my mind, I sat there shocked. I had forgotten that memory until I heard the whispered,

Remember when. I sat in stunned silence and let the memory wash over me. This opened the floodgates of revelation with respect to my and Michael's intertwined lives. So many things immediately flooded my consciousness, it was overwhelming. Everyone who knew Michael and I understood there was something special between us, more than just mother and son. Our bond was extraordinarily connected, as ordained by God, and it was all rapidly firing back into my consciousness through these memories.

That long-ago morning when Michael, as a very young child, told me forth-right he was murdered, in my spirit I knew there was something not right about his ability to articulate a thought such as that. From that moment on, I was always fearful in my spirit for Michael, throughout his entire life, and I couldn't understand why. As time went on, the conscious memory of that day faded. Day after day, year after year, every time I heard an ambulance, my mind jumped to the proximity of where Michael was in relation to the sound of the siren. It was always so unsettling. Now I understood why - my spirit knew - there was a catastrophic destiny preordained for the end of his life.

As I sat there with these thoughts cascading over me, I gazed towards his urn and my spirit was awakened with knowledge and confirmation. I had a small glass container sitting inside a metal stand at the base of Michael's urn - one of the many small gifts that were given to us when Michael died. On my coffee table I had a round candle, the size that fit snugly in the top of the glass container. I previously had no reason to connect the two items, but I slowly took the candle and set it on the glass container, igniting another shocking memory. The candle I placed atop the glass container sitting in the metal stand, looked very similar to, but much smaller than, the pedestal I had been standing in front of before I was born!

My memory was flashing now, and I recalled being told of death and that I would lose someone close to me, but at that time I didn't have any understanding or concept of death. I remembered that I arrogantly said it would, *be a breeze* and I felt I could get easily get through the pending earth test. I now understood losing Michael was part of my life test! I further recalled my conversation with Pastor Cataudella when I was seeking advice in my lack of emotional devastation when Michael died, and her words that the gift of God's grace and His peace that surpasses all understanding was what covered me in my grief.

I remembered my dad's words from his letter in January 2005: "You, as any child, are blessed with the knowledge of all this world upon your birth and although you seem to "lose" it as age progresses, you do not, it is still in your subconscious and in time of extreme need it will come back to you as much as it is required at that time."

My subconscious mind was now awakened by the Holy Spirit to the incredible story of Michael's and mine interwoven purpose, which is to share God's glory with the retelling to you. I am surely blessed that God has chosen me to reveal His power and authority. Sarah's words from the night Michael died resonate in my heart and in my spirit: "Yes we were blessed. We had Michael for 25 years!"

So many things made sense to me now. I now understood why I was not laid out in absolute, devastating grief. I had grieved Michael in my spirit since the day as a child he told me, "Mommy, I've been murdered!" It was almost as if my spirit was released, at peace from the secret it had held those many years. It was now God's time for all things to be revealed to me.

I share with you my clear understanding that, *my breeze,* spoken of before I was born, was and is *God's grace and mercy* through His impartation of peace that surpasses all understanding!

Blessed Lord, I thank You for leading me through this path You have ordained for me.

Count Your Blessings

What shall I render to the Lord *For* all His benefits toward me? - Psalm 116:12

The Easter preceding Michael's death, before we had returned to attending church, our family was enjoying the season as many families did, but unfortunately without the acknowledgement and celebration of the glorious sacrifice given by our Lord. We had been invited to my brother Kevin's house for Easter dinner. It was a great day of eating and sharing stories, particularly for the benefit of Chanel, Michael's girlfriend. We had lots of stories to share about growing up in our household and were giving her a hilarious, bird's-eye view of what she was getting into in by joining our family.

Chanel was having a good time, as we all were, but the visit was peppered by her constant picture taking. I don't think any of us minded a few pictures but she seemed to take an excessive number throughout the day. It struck me as annoying at the time, by the number she was taking, due to the many interruptions. However, since everyone else was having a good time, I did not want to make a fuss about it. I simply thought it was a sign of the times for young people, who always seemed to have a camera ready on their phone, and to be constantly taking pictures.

I came to regret that I had felt annoyed by the picture taking. As it turned out, the many pictures she took are the last pictures we have of Michael with the family; during that Easter get together. A plethora of pictures were taken: Michael and I, Michael and his dad, Michael and Sarah, Michael and his uncle Kevin, Michael and Chanel. The pictures show everyone so happy and enjoying each other. Had Chanel not taken those pictures, we would not have had them to cherish and enjoy and remember our last joyful get-together as a family with Michael present.

One of these pictures in particular has special honour in my heart; it is the last picture taken of Michael and I before he died. This picture was chosen to adorn the CD of his love song to me, "I Love You Mama." Had God not ordained His favour and orchestrated our family day together, including Chanel's incessant picture taking, I would not have this forever reminder of my darling son and I on his CD, to love and cherish forever.

"Thank You, Father, for showing me Your mercy and loving-kindness at a time when I didn't deserve, acknowledge or celebrate Your great sacrifice of giving Your Only Son that I should live. Nor did I recognize Your handiwork of love for my future, to celebrate Michael and my love through his CD adorned with our last picture together.

Understanding God's Sacrifice

For God so loved the world that He gave His only begotten Son, that whoever believes in Him should not perish but have everlasting life. - John 3:16

What a difference a year makes. The Easter following Michael's death I was heavily involved in the church and living a life of getting to know the Bible. Although I had accepted the Lord on that Easter service long ago as a child, and again when I joined the church as a young adult, I had not been baptized since I was a baby in my mother's arms. Now there I was, as previously stated, planning on being baptized at the end of April 2008, to proclaim my life as Jesus's. Additionally, my immediate family and my niece had accepted Christ, and God was strengthening and spiritually comforting us in our loss. I had found my church family and found a real sense of spiritual family once more.

This Easter, after losing Michael, I was led to really scrutinize for the first time, the love of God's sacrifice in giving His Son for my sins so that I could claim everlasting life through His resurrection. How many times had I recited John 3:16 scripture in my lifetime? Too many times to remember and recall. Like you, I knew the words. I recited the words countless times, but until then I couldn't begin to comprehend the extraordinary love, sacrifice and grace of God. Now this scripture *breathed* and became alive to me. I have an extraordinary hard time reconciling the scope and depth of His love for me by giving His Son, after I experienced the devastating death of my precious son. This scripture struck my heart; the infinite capacity of His love for me, so hard to comprehend in my human existence and experience.

"He gave His only begotten Son" – The words *He gave,* rang in my ears. How could that be? His sacrifice so unimaginable, so selfless, so magnificent, I cannot fathom in a million lifetimes. God is so perfect that only He could give His Son for ransom for undeserving, unworthy me. Reflecting on my loss of Michael, in my human state, I wondered, *Would I, could I be so selfless to give such love away, for any reason for any purpose?* A resounding no! On the contrary, I would give absolutely anything to have my boy back with me. The very thought that God gave His Son for me is impossible for me to understand, comprehend, reconcile or digest in my life, especially in light of my own unfit existence and experience of loss. God's all-consuming love was, and is, truly inconceivable in the natural. Until I lost my own son, so precious, this scripture was totally beyond my scope of reasoning. I now have a deeper, more personal understanding of the gravity of God's sacrifice.

The magnificence of His love is still beyond my natural understanding, but I humbly and gloriously accept Jesus as my Lord and Saviour. I accept the greatest gift, He so gave, so that I could be called and live eternal life with Him, in His kingdom. Hallelujah!

CHAPTER 7

Blessed Assurance

"Ask, and it will be given to you; seek, and you will find; knock, and it will be opened to you." - Matthew 7:7

Big things, little things, many things - it doesn't seem to matter why or how God chooses to manifest His presence in the lives of those He so desires.

One morning I had an occasion to go to the Centenary Hospital in Scarborough, for an X-ray when I saw a woman sitting alone in the busy Admission Reception area. Why she stood out to me I didn't know, but I noticed she was well dressed and about my age. I made my way to register for my X-ray, and once my registration was completed, I was directed to where I should go.

I was concerned for my well-being and the reason that the doctor had scheduled the X-ray. It didn't take long to have the X-ray done. As I left the X-ray area and walked down the corridor, I came upon the hospital chapel, went inside, and said a prayer for healing. As I prayed, the lady I had noticed sitting outside in the reception area came to mind, and I said a prayer for her as well.

As I was about to leave the hospital, I had to pass back by the reception area and she was still sitting there alone. Why was this total stranger on my mind? It was baffling to me, but I continued on my way toward the hospital exit. Before I reached it, I thought,

I should go back and pray with her. I was not prompted by a voice or a whisper this time; she was just heavy on my mind since I first saw her earlier that day. I also wondered if she would be receptive to a stranger's intrusion of her waiting for whatever reason brought her to the hospital.

As I turned back and walked over to her, I wondered what would I say so she wouldn't think I had lost my mind. When I got to her, I sat in the seat next to her and turned in my seat to face her, and she looked at me. I smiled and asked her if she would like to pray with me. She said, "Thank you Jesus," and then, "Yes." We held hands and prayed a short healing prayer for her situation. When we were finished praying, I got up to leave, but she held out her hand to stop me and thanked me for asking to pray with her. She did not share what brought her to the hospital, but she said she had been so afraid about a procedure she had to undergo that day. She told me, as she sat there waiting and anxious, she had been praying to Jesus to give her a sign that all would be well. My surprising request to stop and ask her to pray was a bigger sign than she had been expecting. Together, we marveled at the wonder of Jesus.

Before parting ways, we hugged across the seats where we sat, and I got up and left, knowing this was the reason she had captured and held my attention when I entered the hospital. Once more, I thanked God for using me in His divine plans for someone else. He has given me a spirit of obedience to do the things He calls me to do, the outcomes of which, increase my desire to hear His voice and do His will when called upon. *There are no coincidences in Christ.*

I Saw What You Did

"Then the righteous will answer Him, saying, 'Lord, when did we see You hungry and feed *You*, or thirsty and give *You* drink?" - Matthew 25:37

One sunny summer Sunday in 2008, driving alone on my way to church. As I was coming off the 401 Highway, I saw a bundle of clothes laying propped up against a traffic pole. Clearly a person was under the bundle, but the person wasn't moving; for a fleeting moment, I wondered if he was dead. When the light changed and I was able to turn the corner in traffic to continue to church, I did so. Before I got very far, the Lord in His mercy for this person, told me in my spirit to *Go back.* I did not want to turn back. I did not want to listen to the voice. I did not want to be late for church. I was looking forward to the service and the worship and I just wanted to be on my way. For several blocks as I continued to drive, I reasoned to myself, *Maybe it was just me,* and not a real prompting to go back. I was in an internal battle, looking for excuses not to turn around, until I was prompted again, *Go back and check on the man.* The Spirit always has a way of making me be obedient to the whispers in my heart, so I finally gave in and said out loud, "Ok, I'll go back." I continued driving to the next block where I could turn around. I figured I had better hurry and get this done so I wouldn't be any later than I had to be for church.

I was several blocks away from the person by now but I turned my car around in a service station. I figured if the person was alive, he'd be hungry. Expecting him to be alive, I went into the kiosk and bought a sandwich, a bottle of water and a bag of chips. I got in my car and drove back to where this person lay. The flow of the traffic was such that I had to drive past him and turn around so I could stop my car on the side of the road beside him.

I stopped my car and put on my hazard lights because the intersection at Kennedy Road and the highway was busy, with all the traffic coming off the highway, and the street being a major artery. I got out of my car and approached the person who I could now see was, in fact, a man. I told him I had passed him moments before and thought he might be hungry and bought him something to eat.

He raised himself up. He was unkempt and dirty, but as he lifted his head, he looked straight at me. His eyes met mine, and

I was drawn into their depth. His eyes were crystal clear and seem to sparkle and he looked directly into my eyes. It was a truly divine moment and I felt like I was looking into the eyes of Jesus. I asked him his name, and he said his name was Rob. I handed Rob the food I had purchased and told him to take care of himself.

Now that I had done my duty as prompted by the Holy Spirit, I just wanted to get to church because I felt that, with all the time I had taken, I surely must be late.

As I drove into the parking lot of the church, there were still people milling around outside, so I breathed a sigh of relief because I knew I had made it in time for the service. It perplexed me that I had arrived so early, after all the time I had spent on the road attending to the prompting to attend to Rob. For a quick second, I entertained the thought that perhaps God had stopped time for Rob. With this nonsensical thought in mind, I was smiling as I walked into the reception area until I noticed a young Black man intently staring at me. I went directly into the sanctuary to find a seat and within a few moments this same young man came and sat in the same pew I was in. I thought, *Oh no*. My husband was not with me this day and I figured, here I was a young woman, alone, and this young man was going to try to talk to me.

I deliberately did not turn in his direction, but out of my peripheral vision I could see him watching me. A few moments passed, then he said, in a deep rich voice, "I saw what you did." My heart started to pound. I turned toward him, and he repeated, "I saw what you did, I saw you feed that homeless man." He told me he had been driving by when he saw me handing the bag of food to the homeless man. He went on to say, "I just want you to know that you blessed me this morning by what you did." I was taken aback. I had no way to know he or anyone else had observed or paid attention to my interaction with Rob. In my surprised state, I quietly mumbled, "Thank you and to God be all the glory!" I was ashamed that I had first thought this young man was trying to converse with me on a social level, when in fact he simply wanted to share how my actions had blessed him.

My heart was still pounding; in my spirit I knew that God sent this young man *to me,* to let me know He had seen my offering to Rob. I immediately thought of the prompting of the Spirit to make me go back and give him some food. I remembered Rob's deep, crystal-clear eyes, and the special moment that I felt passed between us. This experience was divinely inspired and connected, and once more the Father used me for His purpose.

After this first chance meeting, I often looked for Rob at that intersection and he would often be at the same spot. I saw him so often, I began to stop for food before I got onto the highway, ready to pass it out to him as I drove by. After a while, and several meetings, I believe he began to look for me on Wednesdays, as I went to Bible study, and Sundays as I went to church. I looked forward to seeing Rob and helping him, even a little bit, by offering him food and a wee chat.

I told my husband about my many encounters with Rob, and eventually we were travelling together and Ed got to meet Rob too. Sometime much later, we came off the highway and saw that a different man was where Rob usually was. Ed comically and surprisingly said, "That's not Rob," as though this new person was an interloper or an imposter. Sure enough, it wasn't Rob. I haven't seen Rob since the encounter before that, but every time I come off the highway at Kennedy Road, I think of him and wonder whatever happened to him. I was truly blessed by meeting him and thank God for extending His love to Rob, through me, in such a charitable way.

We serve an almighty God!

God Encircles His Children

"For where two or three are gathered together in My name, I am there in the midst of them." - Matthew 18:20

God brings His children together for love, comfort and support. This became more and more evident at my workplace as time went on. It began with Judy years before and I soon became bolder in my declaration of loving Christ due to His mercy for me in Michael's passing. I now took every opportunity presented by the Father to pray with, and for, others. I didn't particularly feel I always articulated the best words of prayer, but I did have the desire to reach out, to intercede, on behalf of others and many would come to me to pray with, and for, them. I was amazed by the number of individuals who declared their love of Christ when given the opportunity, and took on a willingness to pray with me, not only for our own wishes, needs, and desires but for others in our workplace and family circles.

I enjoyed a very strong prayer time with my wonderful church partners, and of course my family. But what struck me was how the Spirit of God began to wonderfully manifest in my workplace through prayer. God began to reveal to us, His children, to one another as Christians. At Centennial College we were provided a safe haven to be comfortable praying and speaking His name. We acknowledged and understood our privilege, that what we experienced openly, may not have been tolerated in other settings and were grateful we had Him and through Him, one another.

We rejoiced in the comfort of one another as Christians. I've shared some names of those who have made themselves available for prayer at my workplace in specific accounts of this book thus far; Georgiana, Judy, and Jenny. Some other names are yet to come, Mede, Ahmed and Malcolm. But one particular prayer warrior in our midst was a close colleague, Nadine. Although Nadine, in her work position reported to me, in the kingdom of God she taught me so much. Nadine's prayers were heavenly inspired, and I remain humbled by the love that she set forth in her desire to intercede to our Father on behalf of myself and others.

Nadine's inspired prayers came forth lovingly from her heart and at all times honoured the Lord Jesus and His majesty in all things, through scriptural references and quotations. By Nadine's actions, I was made stronger in my faith, and I will always cherish her love of Christ and the light she shined in our midst.

Forerunner Vision

But as for me, I will walk in my integrity; Redeem me and be merciful to me. - Psalm 26:11

As a young girl I had grown up surreptitiously hearing stories of "forerunners of death," from the older people. No small wonder I had been afraid of the dark. My parents shared many of the stories when they were entertaining; having friends over and reminiscing about the things they had encountered when they were growing up or were passed down from their parents. These stories were frightening and not meant for us children to hear, but as children sometimes do, we would stay awake and listen, when we were supposed to be fast asleep.

Driving to work as usual one morning, I became distressed to see a vision in the air, elevated in front of me through the windshield. This vision showed my mother and my sister, Lynn, walking toward me, both of them clothed in long dark coats that reached to the ground. They were not crying or outwardly distraught, but both of them appeared downcast and sad. I mentioned to Sarah who was driving with me, that I had to call her grandmother when I got to work because something was wrong and I told her what I had just seen before me in the sky.

When I got to work, I called my mother only to learn a dear family friend, George, had taken ill, was in the hospital and was not expected to live much longer. George was a longstanding family friend with strong ties particularly to my mother and my sister. Unfortunately, George died two days later.

My vision of seeing my mom and my sister walking toward me as I drove to work was the first, and only time I had personally experienced a forerunner of death. Why I was linked to George in such as manner I never quite figured out. I had been away from home for some 29 years, when this occurred and George, although he always referred to me as "Princess," was devoted to my mom and my sister. I am therefore more convinced I experienced this forerunner of George's death because of the imminent loss my mom and sister were soon to experience due to his passing, rather than being linked to him directly.

This remains a mystery I cannot explain.

Ghostly Visitor Returns

Examine me, O Lord, and prove me; Try my mind and my heart. - Psalm 26:2

Michael's ashes were kept in an urn on a pedestal in the white room. We had prepared a memorial to him, and around the urn were pictures of Michael, tokens of love and keepsakes from friends and family. Behind the pedestal was a large earthen pitcher filled with a large sky-blue flower arrangement, Michael's favourite colour.

This is where Sarah experienced her last sighting of the little blond girl's ghost. Sarah was coming down the stairs leading to our French doors into the white room. As she descended the stairs, she said she saw Michael's spirit sitting on the lower steps, peering through the glass of the French doors, looking into the white room. Michael's spirit appeared to be looking in the direction of his urn.

As Sarah went further down the stairs, she followed his gaze and saw the little blond girl's spirit standing beside Michael's urn and the memorial we had set up. Sarah said the girl's spirit appeared to be very interested in this new development in the house. By the time Sarah reached the bottom of the stairs, both spirits had vanished. This was the last time either Sarah, or I, saw the little blonde girl's ghost.

But God, I Don't Want to Write a Book!

God First, Then You

Trust in the Lord with all your heart, And lean not on your own understanding; In all your ways acknowledge Him, and He shall direct your paths. - Proverbs 3:5-6

Through the next few stories regarding Phyllis, Norma and Jenny, I have the dates of occurrence because I was so astonished by what I was experiencing that I started to write segments of this book as they occurred. I note also that the dates are important and God has a way of ensuring His message is delivered in the context He desires to glorify His plan. I am glad I began to write and you will see through the supernatural weaving of events, the fruition of His awesome design on many levels and through a number of stages.

Early in April 2012, I was driving home and had an overwhelming and joyful desire to do something good for someone. I have often felt the urge to do something specific in my spirit, but this was more of a "general" do something, and I had never experienced this before.

As I continued on, singing along with the worship music in my car, was not really paying much attention to the, "doing something good," but as I got nearer to my house, I saw a lady who is often out in the neighbourhood. I don't believe she is homeless, but she certainly seems down on her luck. I often see her looking in garbage receptacles, and on two previous occasions I had given her a small gift of money in passing.

When I saw her, I thought, *Here is my opportunity to do something good.* But I only had twenty dollars in my wallet and I selfishly, didn't want to give it all to her, so I drove past her and talked to myself, making a deal about giving her the money. As it happens, I was expecting my income tax cheque and a work expense cheque in the mail any day, so I bargained, *If any of the cheques have arrived, I would drive back and give her the twenty dollars.* When I got to my mailbox, there were no cheques in the mail, and I thought, *Good, I get to keep my twenty dollars.* But the Holy Spirit spoke to me and said, "It means more to give, when you give all you have." Knowing the voice of the Spirit, I responded, "Okay," got back in my car and turned around to go back to give her the twenty dollars.

At first, I didn't see her and again thought, *Good, I get to keep my twenty dollars.* But sure enough, I looked up a side street and there she was heading in the opposite direction. No one else was on the street and I didn't want her to be afraid of this woman, me, approaching her in a car. So, I drove my car past her, and parked and walked back to her so she could see me coming towards her. I smiled and as I got close to her, I reached out my hand, sure by this time she recognized me. I had previously given her loose change on a couple of occasions. I handed her the twenty dollars. I was proud of myself being obedient to the prompting of the Spirit. She obviously possesses very little. She gave me a big smile and said, "Thank you," and I said, "Thank God." She pointed to the sky and said, "God first, then you," and I laughed and repeated, "Yes, God first, then me." I put my arm around her shoulder and said, "You know God loves you." She repeated "God first, then you."

My arm was still around her shoulder and I said, "My name is Scherry." I was prompted to tell her my name was Grace, to reflect God's goodness and so as not to take credit for my offering to her, but I didn't, and I regret not doing so. I asked her, "What is your name?" and she said, "Phyllis" and then she said, "Italian." I assumed she said that to let me know she couldn't converse with me. So, I repeated, "God loves you," gave her a hug and I went on my way, truly blessed.

About a week after this meeting with Phyllis, the Holy Spirit impressed upon me to, *Buy her a gift.* I knew the voice but I thought to myself, *Really, why would I buy a gift for this lady I don't know and rarely see?* I reasoned with myself, I had already given her money and that should be the end of it. Indeed, not one of my best moments, but I need to be honest in relaying this story.

Days went by and the urging didn't leave me. I decided I would go buy her a gift, although having no idea when I would see her again. I did not wish to disobey the prompting that I knew was the Holy Spirit. I see her sporadically, a few times a year, but not regularly by any stretch of the imagination. At first, I had no idea what to buy for her, but then I thought to buy a cross, to honour the, "God first, then you" sentiment she had shared. Once the idea of a cross came to me, I envisioned giving her a small glittering cross, in a little square box, that I would safeguard in my glove compartment until I see her.

The Reluctant Gift

The angel of the Lord encamps all around those who fear Him, And delivers them. - Psalm 34:7

Ed and I put a memorial in the obituary section of the paper to commemorate what would have been Michael's thirtieth birthday on April 20, 2012. Two of my church sisters had asked that I get a copy for them as they did not subscribe to the paper. I tried to take photocopies of my original memorial at a local drug store, but the copies didn't come out very well. I simply stuck the poor copies in my purse and purchased two papers, cut out the memorials and gave those to my church sisters.

On April 21, the Saturday following Michael's birthday, we had a small family birthday memorial dinner for him. His aunt Norma and cousin Teesha and her daughters needed a ride to come to our house. Norma would usually drive, but her car was in the shop. I went to pick them all up. On the way back to my house, I asked Norma if she saw the memorial in the paper and she said she had not. I told her I had a copy she could read.

For Michael's memorial dinner, I cooked lasagna, his favourite meal, his Aunt Norma baked ham, another of Michael's favourites and his cousin Teesha baked a birthday cake. As I was setting the table I remembered the memorial, retrieved it, and simply placed in front of Norma, but I didn't say anything. I had just intended to show it to her, for her to read. I continued setting the table. As I was busy getting dinner ready, I noticed Norma read the memorial, then fold it and tuck it in her wallet. This was my original and I really wanted to keep it, but I didn't have the heart to tell her. She too loved Michael so much. I think she mistakenly thought I was giving it to her to keep.

My mind was racing: *Could I ask her for it back*? I really felt kind of sad to give it up, but I was prompted by the Holy Spirit; reminding me that I have Michael in my heart, as well as many pictures and remembrances; I should be generous of spirit and let her keep it. I didn't want to, but the Holy Spirit also reminded me that I still had the copies in my purse, so I reluctantly chose not to ask for it back. Sometimes it is hard to be obedient when your flesh wants to satisfy itself. This was one of those times for me.

After the memorial dinner had ended, Ed left to drive Norma, Teesha and the girls back home. I went to retrieve the poor photocopies, and with a bit of a heavy heart I put one of them with my other keepsakes of Michael, reminding myself that I was surrounded by many possessions related to Michael and I needed to be generous of spirit in letting the original memorial go. It wasn't easy.

God's Reward

Oh, taste and see that the Lord *is* good; Blessed *is* the man *who* trusts in Him! - Psalm 34:8

I was at work on the following Wednesday, April 25, 2012, waiting to speak with a co-worker, Asiye. In the waiting area outside her office, there was a newspaper on the table and because Asiye wasn't ready to see me just yet, I picked it up to read while I waited. I noticed the paper was dated April 20, Michael's birthday. Everyone at the college was so supportive of me in my loss of Michael, especially because everyone knew him and loved him as well, so my first thought was that the newspaper had been placed there deliberately, left for anyone who came in to review his memorial. Suddenly, the other lady in the office, Beth, saw me looking at the paper and she said, "Oh, Scherry, that is an old paper, we've been meaning to throw it out."

At this moment Asiye became available, and I asked the two of them if I could have the paper because Michael's memorial was in it. Of course, they said I could have it. Beth and I followed Asiye's into her office. I had already opened the paper to the memorial page and laid it out on Asiye's desk for them to see. This gave me an opening to talk about my loss and witness to them the goodness of God in my life and how He sustains me with His loving-kindness, His mercy and most of all His grace. I shared with them the stories about Michael prophesying his death when he was little, and about the wall of angels I saw in my dining room, in the days before his funeral.

I always had a wonderful time witnessing about the goodness of God and talking about my Michael. I thanked them for the newspaper and shared that I had reluctantly given my original memorial to my friend Norma. I shared with them how hard I had struggled with my decision to part with the one I let Norma keep; that I had been led to follow the prompting of the Spirit, to be more generous toward her feelings of loss for Michael, because she loved him like her own. I told them how sad I had been to let that original go, but I was being obedient to the prompting of the Holy Spirit. As I was speaking, I realized that God had given me back an original memorial, to replace the one I had given to Norma, through finding this paper that was left in their office! I immediately shared with them that I discerned God had repaid my obedience to give Norma my original memorial by providing this one. I told them I was confident that was the *very reason* why the paper was still there, and had not been not thrown out. I exclaimed, "How great is our God!"

Before I could say anything else Asiye said, "This is no coincidence," to which I replied, "*There are no coincidences in Christ.*"

Upon reflection when writing this book, I had a revelation. I believe God had a much higher purpose for that newspaper to be left there for me to find. It was left there, not to just give me an original copy, His higher purpose was the window He opened, allowing me to witness His divine mercy and grace to my coworkers who may have needed to hear of His majesty from a personal perspective, directly from someone they knew and trusted, who knew and trusted Him!

Thank You, Father, for Your divine orchestration of these events to exalt Your Name.

Phyllis's Cross

Blessed *is* he who considers the poor; The Lord will deliver him in time of trouble. - Psalm 41:1

God continued His unmerited favour. Later the same day, Wednesday, April 25, 2012, during my lunch break, I decided while I had some time, I would go buy the cross I had envisioned for Phyllis. I felt so thankful and so blessed by having the memorial given back to me, I wanted to honour that gift from God by actually buying a gift for Phyllis. I was going to go to a faith bookstore, but I remembered the crosses I had previously seen there, I did not particularly like, so instead I went to the Pickering Town Centre, hoping there would be more options for what I was specifically looking for.

I stopped at one mall jewelry kiosk and a cross sort of caught my eye but it was not the one had I envisioned. I went to another kiosk and they had nothing and I felt a bit disappointed because I knew *exactly* what I was looking for. I returned to the first kiosk and asked about the one I had seen on my way in. It was nice enough, but there was a gem in the middle of the cross where Christ was supposed to be. I didn't really like it but I wanted to follow my spirit to be obedient to buy a gift. I asked the clerk how much it cost and she told me. The chain was one price and the cross was another price and to be honest I had no intention of paying the combined prices she gave me when I thought to buy the gift in the first place.

So once again I thought, *Really, Lord, why am I paying for a gift for this lady I don't even know?"* I am ashamed of my selfish thoughts, but I need to be truthful.

Anyway, I told the salesclerk I would take it, and then she asked me which box I wanted. One was a long box and the other was a hexagon shape. The long box was pretty with a bow, but neither box was the box I had envisioned giving Phyllis. As the lady was cutting off the price tags, she asked me how I was going to pay and I told her it would be debit. Just as she was about to ring up my purchase, I said to her, "I want to check one more place if you don't mind." I was reluctant to say I had changed my mind now that she had started the transaction, but it wasn't what I wanted. She didn't seem too pleased, but I just couldn't buy it, especially with the gem on the middle of the cross. It just was not sitting well in my spirit; it was all wrong. This cross wasn't what I envisioned, the gem in the middle was bothering me and then, the box was all wrong, so I walked away from the purchase.

I left that kiosk and went farther into the mall to a Swarovski store. I was looking around and had lost hope, when there it was - the exact cross I had envisioned! It cost one dollar more than the combined cross and chain I had almost purchased at the kiosk. As I said, I had not intended to pay this amount but I was over asking why I was spending this much; I knew I had to be obedient and buy it because I knew I had been led to this cross. The clerk put it in a box but I was dismayed that the box was not the box I envisioned. She asked if I wanted it gift wrapped but I chose not to, not quite knowing what I would do at this point about the box.

That evening I had a wonderful time of prayer alone, Ed and Sarah were not at home, so it was quiet time to spend with God.

Later, as I was getting ready for bed, the Holy Spirit let me know that I could not give the cross to her in a box that was labelled "Swarovski" because this gift was not about Swarovski, it was about God. Now I had a dilemma: what would I put the cross in to give to Phyllis? I prayed about what to do and then left the issue alone until I could think of something.

That night I remembered a cross that had been given to me the previous Christmas by my daughter Sarah and that it had been in a small, black, felt carrying bag. The bag was not what I had envisioned either, but I thought, *Great I will give it to her in this nice bag,* even though I would have to find something nice to put Sarah's cross in for safekeeping. In my mind, it was far better than the box with *Swarovski* written across it.

God had another plan.

But God, I Don't Want to Write a Book!

Rejoice always, pray without ceasing, in everything give thanks: for this is the will of God in Christ Jesus concerning you. - 1 Thessalonians 5:16-18

When I woke up in the morning of Friday, April 27th, 2012, there was a sense of urgency in my spirit about the cross telling me, *Wrap it up, put it in the felt bag and put it in your purse.* I followed the insistence of the prompting, and before I left for work, I prepared it and put it in my purse.

Jenny had been on vacation in Greece to visit her aging Orthodox Christian parents. Her parents have since passed away, may they rest in peace and in the loving comfort of Christ. While Jenny was in Greece, she texted me that she had lit a candle for Michael on his birthday, April 20. She returned to work on Friday, April 27. I still had Michael's memorial on my desk that I received from Asiye, and I took it to Jenny's desk to show her because she loved Michael and hadn't seen it. I had witnessed to Jenny on numerous occasions since we prayed that first day, five years previously. I am always happy to share with Jenny the blessing that God provides to me, first because I am so blessed, second, to confirm His working goodness in my life and third, to encourage her.

I shared with her the workings that God had orchestrated to give Michael's memorial back to me through Asiye; a testament to His acknowledgement for my obedience in giving my original to Norma. Jenny got teary-eyed and I left her desk to give her privacy and so we both could get back to work.

About a half an hour later, Jenny stepped into my office with a gift for me she had purchased while in Greece. She gave me a cross! Not only had He gifted me the memorial through Asiye, God had through Jenny, rewarded my obedience in purchasing a cross for Phyllis, by having Jenny purchase a cross for me.

I knew this was His confirmation to me that I had obeyed His Spirit to honour Phyllis for His purpose. "Thank You Father!" As I shared early on in this book, some of these events are so fantastical that I sometimes doubt myself and what I am experiencing, but He confirms every time, in some way, what I have done has been performed at His urging.

Jenny giving me the cross gave me a blessed opportunity to witness to her the correlation of my purchasing a cross for Phyllis, and her role in God's plans. It was a bigger correlation than I first thought. Jenny went on to share with me that the cross she gave me, was not the original cross she had purchased! She said the cross she originally purchased, did not sit well with her, reminding me of the first cross I almost purchased for Phyllis, did not sit well with me. Jenny said she went back the next day, returned the first cross and purchased the cross she gave to me! Jenny was prompted to go back for the cross she gave me because I believe she was being obedient to a prompting her spirit, and in doing so completed God's task for her in this situation.

Incredibly, the cross Jenny gave me was in a small box, the

very box I had envisioned for Phyllis's cross! God in His infinite plan had provided the small box for Phyllis's cross. Through Jenny's obedience of listening and acting on her prompting by the Holy Spirit, He gifted me a cross and gave me the box for Phyllis. *There are no coincidences in Christ Jesus!*

I promptly took the cross for Phyllis out of the felt bag that was still in my purse and put Phyllis's cross in the box from Jenny and put the box in my purse for whenever I see Phyllis. I shared with Jenny her role in this blessing including the significance of the box her cross came in. Jenny left my office literally shaking and marveling in the extravagant orchestration undertaken by our Lord and Saviour, for us each to do the things He designs.

I give thanks for a wonderful testimony that only God could provide. His Hand is woven through all these interconnected experiences in a way that only can be explained through Him. *Praise Your Holy Name, and thank You Father for blessing me with this testimony to share.*

He wasn't done. The next day, on April 28, 2012, a Saturday, I went into the office to do some work, and the plan I had in the back of my mind was, that if I had time, I would write down the testimony I have given above while it was still fresh in my mind. The circumstances were too fantastic not to record them. The work took longer than I expected, and once I finished, I did not want to take the time, just then, to write down the testimony. I knew it would take a significant amount of time and at this point, I simply wanted to go home. I thought, *I will record these happenings during the coming week on my lunch hour breaks,* but the Spirit was nagging at me to start it. I didn't want to, but I knew I had to be obedient. When I got the first sentence started, I went back to the top of the page and wrote the title: *But God, I Don't Want To Write A Book!*

The title was apropos, I really didn't *want* to write a book, but ultimately this was to be my destiny, as ordained by my Heavenly Father, and thus became the title. That is the reason I have the specific dates for these events; I started to write some of these events at this time as prompted by the Holy Spirit. I contacted Georgiana and told her, "I started writing the book!"

God was enduring in His plan to bring this book to fruition.

Cross Finale

Now may the God of hope fill you with all joy and peace in believing, that you may abound in hope by the power of the Holy Spirit. - Romans 15:13

Sunday, April 29, 2012, I was on my way home from church and I stopped at a takeout to pick up lunch for the family. As I was waiting in the car for my order, the Spirit suddenly prompted me to question myself, *Where is the cross?* With a sense of urgency, I started rummaging through my purse in a bit of a panic, I didn't remember what I had done with it! My heart was beating rapidly, *Where is the cross!* Eventually, I found the box in a zippered part of my purse, let out a sigh of relief, and I said a prayer of thanks for finding it and I put it in my glove box as was originally intended, saying to the Lord, *There, it's in the glove box for whenever I see Phyllis.* My food order came and I drove off toward home.

As I was driving down the street, I saw an elderly white-haired lady with a wheeled walker going very slowly down the road. When I passed her, I realized no matter where she was going, she had a long way to walk. She was on a long stretch of road without any houses or businesses nearby. I thought I should stop to help her, but I kept going. I got about a block past her and the Spirit urged me, *Go back for her.* As was my pattern, I didn't want to go back. I had our warm lunch in my car and was mentally making a case that the food would get cold. But recognizing the voice, I said, "Okay Lord," and I turned my car around.

I drove past her and turned into an industrial driveway. By the time I pulled into the driveway and parked and she was slowly passing by behind my car and I walked over to her. I said to her, "You seem to be going pretty slow and wherever you are heading you may have quite a distance to go. Would you like a lift?" She said, "Oh God love you," and graciously accepted. She said was on her way to a shower and she had been waiting and waiting for the bus, but no bus came, so she started to walk because she did not want to be late.

I asked her name and she responded, "Ruth," and I introduced myself. I asked her if her walker folded and she said it did, so I folded it and put it in the trunk and then helped her into the car. In the car she repeated, "Oh God love you." I said to her, "God must really love you because He made me turn around and come back for you." We drove down the street; she said was going to the McLean Community Centre for the shower. Just as I turned the corner to go into the community centre, who did I see in the parking lot, but Phyllis?! The Holy Spirit prompting me, as I waited for my food order, to quickly locate the cross, confirmed without a doubt, *this was no coincidence!*

I immediately knew God put Ruth in my path because if I hadn't listened to the prompting of the Spirit to go back to pick her up, I would not have seen Phyllis. I had no business in the community centre, and would have no reason to turn that corner on my way home. I shook my head and internally laughed at the way God works His wonders as I continued driving into the community centre parking lot to drop Ruth off. When she got out of the car, she repeated, "God love you," and after I retrieved her walker out of the trunk, she went into the centre to attend her shower on time.

I was beyond elated. I was then on a mission to see Phyllis and give her the cross, knowing this was all God's doing! I pulled around in the parking lot and at first, I did not see her. After surveying the area, finally, there she was. She had walked out the community centre parking lot and across the road into the shopping centre parking lot. I opened my glove compartment and got the box to give to her.

I drove across to the shopping centre, stepped out of my car and

I approached her with the box, thinking she would remember me. I smiled, but she did not smile back. I realized she didn't recognize me; at least there was no glimmer of recognition indicating that she did. I held out the box to her and she gestured and said, "No, no money." I said to her, "It is a gift from God, remember, 'God first, then me?'" I was trying to spark her memory of our last encounter, but she didn't respond as though she remembered. I gave her the box and told her to put it in her bag and open it when she got home. I am not sure she understood, but she took the box and said, "Thank you." I got in my car and drove home. That was the last time I ever saw Phyllis.

I was happy because I knew for whatever purpose, this series of numerous "chance meetings" and actions were ordained by God. He chooses me in these "missions," by giving me a spirit of obedience, as He has done on so many occasions; to bless others and at the same time mightily blessing me. I am thankful for His gift of an obedient spirit that is receptive to the promptings of the Holy Spirit, to perform His will in all these instances of love and mercy.

God had one more gift to present in this fantastic saga, His most precious gift!

Jenny Saved

'And it shall come to pass That whoever calls on the name of the LORD Shall be saved.' - **Acts 2:21**

Jenny and I became much closer friends after Michael died. I was drawn to her because she had shown so much love for Michael as they had become close by working together. We now prayed often for many things, including health, particularly her cancer journey, our families and our lives. We shared lots of memories, including the extraordinary interwoven cross saga.

Over the years, I was prompted by the Holy Spirit on a number of occasions, to ask Jenny if she wanted to give her life to the Jesus.

She declined on these many occasions, saying she was scared. I told her it was not something to be afraid of, quite the contrary, it was something wonderful and to be celebrated. Jenny was the first person I ever asked if they wanted to accept Christ as their Lord and Saviour. I didn't feel I knew what I was doing, but I trusted in the Lord to lead me in the path He wanted me to go.

On Monday, April 30, 2012, I went to work and began sharing my story with Jenny about the culmination of this saga; what had transpired the day before regarding picking up Ruth, which led me to see Phyllis and give her the cross. It was amazing, and because of the cross and the box Jenny had given to me, she too was a part of this epic story. When I finished telling Jenny about what transpired with Ruth and Phyllis, she said she had goosebumps and that she believed in God. The Holy Spirit prompted me, *Ask her if she wants to accept Jesus*, so I said to her, "You know Jenny you can pray anytime, you don't need me." I was attempting to deflect the prompting, reluctant to ask her the big question again. The Spirit prompted me again, *Ask her*. It was more compelling this time, so I asked her, "Jenny are you ready to accept Jesus into your life?" She said, "I am scared," and I replied, "Jesus is love, and there is no reason to be scared." Then, Jenny said, "Yes!"

She was ready.

I retrieved the copy of the Sinner's Prayer I carried in my purse. With Jenny and I sitting facing one another she recited the prayer after me and accepted Christ in her life at that moment. Hallelujah!

When we were done praying, she cried and said she was happy she had made the decision to give herself to God. I felt overwhelmed with gratitude. The Lord, who had not only given the gift of salvation to Jenny but appointed me to be the one that the Holy Spirit designated to lead her to Jesus.

It took almost five years of the work of the Holy Spirit to bring Jenny to the Lord; from that first prayer after I crossed the college entrance bridge after Michael died in 2007 and the Lord told me, *Pray for Jenny*, to this day she accepted Christ. When we are obedient the Lord and Saviour, He will work His miracles through our lives, by His design in His time.

Not long after Jenny accepted Christ, she shared with me that her family recently revealed to her that, when she was diagnosed with cancer in 2002, that the doctor had given her 6 months to live. At the time neither her doctors nor her family told her about this, wanting to protect her. It would have been too upsetting for her. I believe it was all part of the Lord's plan and He healed her the day we first prayed together. As I write this at the end of 2020, Jenny is a saved and highly-favoured child of God, 18 years after the dire diagnosis.

What an awesome God we serve!

CHAPTER 8

God Manifested Good

But as for you, you meant evil against me, *but* God meant it for good, in order to bring it about *as it is* this day, to save many people alive. - Genesis 50:20

I went to Bible study in May 2012, the week following the day Jenny accepted Christ. I was sharing with the group the blessing of Jenny accepting the Lord Jesus and the blessing the Father gave me to lead her in the Sinner's Prayer. I was also sharing my joy and relationship with Christ, through my blessing that Michael had been my son, as I did at every opportunity I found. I was speaking about the Lord's grace in preserving my sanity and holding up our family. I expressed that my one question for God was - why Michael was allowed to be taken that horrific way? I told them about the bad car accident Michael had been in the spring of that year and explained how he came out of that accident without a scratch, even though he had totaled his dad's brand-new car. As any mother would be, I was so thankful that God had spared Michael's life the day of the accident, but I questioned why he had to be murdered that terrible way.

As grossly abnormal as it seems, I remember an inexplicable feeling of elation the week leading up to Michael's funeral, as though I was expecting a great gift. I couldn't reconcile this feeling to any normal, expected emotion of grief, especially by the way in which he died. Grief is starkly incomprehensible in the moment.

After Bible study, I had offered sister Lydia, one of my church sisters a drive home to her house. As we drove, we talked about our relationship with Christ and shared some of the challenges and heartaches we both had encountered in life with our respective sons. In my situation, Lydia pointed out that God often turns bad things for good. She went on to say, since Michael's death, many of my family members had been saved. She suggested others might be saved through my family's witnessing of our personal relationships with Christ; other souls could possibly be drawn to Christ and salvation through our testimonies. At the time, I thought sister Lydia was speaking of those individuals who shot Michael, and I glibly responded, "I don't think we run in the same circles." I knew in my heart that whoever was responsible for Michael's death needed the Lord's compassion as much as I, but I wasn't thinking about them at that time.

I did not understand at first, the significance of what she had said. The *why* Michael died was not answered for me through my dear sister, but the answer to "Why did he have to die *that way?*" was soon to be prompted by the Holy Spirit. Through sister Lydia's comment, she had opened a window of reflection and allowed me to see how God turns tragedy into blessings.

During my morning devotion the following Sunday, May 5, 2012, God provided confirmation of my sister's suggestion through my daily scripture reading, which happened to be, Genesis 50:20. This provided an understanding to comfort my heart concerning why Michael died *the way* he did. I believe, through our family's heart-breaking loss of Michael and the following trauma of dealing with his tragic death, we required a deeper comfort and sought the ultimate solace from our Lord; He had called us to His kingdom through salvation. What greater gift is there than salvation?

It was spiritually revealed that, had Michael died in the spring car accident, although our family would certainly have deeply mourned his loss and passing, we would not have been so absolutely broken and so utterly devastated that we would seek God's comfort in the same way we did after he died so horrifically. God did not take my son away from me, but God turned evil into good - that through Michael's death, God in His infinite mercy drew me and the rest of my family and others closer to His breast and to His kingdom of everlasting life.

Sister Lydia's comments helped me to see and accept in my spirit that Michael's death, as traumatic as it was, ultimately led to the salvation of me and my family. Over time, the Lord blessed me in allowing me to lead not only my friend Jenny, but also another friend and my dad - prior to his being called home to glory last year - in the Sinner's Prayer to their salvation. How magnificent His love is for us all!

Thank You, Father, for wrapping me in Your arms, and comforting my spirit this way, spoken through my dear church sister and confirmed through Your scripture.

Toonie on the Floor

So He said, "Truly I say to you that this poor widow has put in more than all; for all these out of their abundance have put in offerings for God, but she out of her poverty put in all the livelihood that she had." - Luke 21:3-4

I was humbled and gently chastised by the Holy Spirit one fine Sunday as I was attending our KRCC church service. Our church community was located in a financially challenged neighbourhood. Many of our congregants relied on fixed incomes through pensions, social assistance, or in some instances, no income at all. Comparatively, God blessed me with a good job and a substantial income as He did for a few others in a position of relative prosperity to the community we all served.

I was proud to tithe my income and often internally patted myself on the back for my faithfulness and generosity. I felt I was doing a great service in sharing the wealth that the Lord had blessed me. Of course, I did not share my act of tithing with my church brothers and sisters, but shamefully in my heart, I felt this sense of superiority every time I made my offering.

The Lord has a way of humbling His children when we are doing things outside His desire for us and He did so for me in this situation. This Sunday, as I sat I my pew and the ushers were preparing to take up the offering, a church member sitting in front of me who was of little financial means was also preparing her offering in anticipation of the ushers coming up the aisle. Suddenly I heard a tinkling under her chair, and when I looked down there it was, she had dropped her offering, a toonie. My heart jumped as I immediately remembered the scripture, as noted at the beginning of this story; the widow who gave all she had, amid those who had more to give, yet didn't. I was also reminded of my own experience earlier, when the Holy Spirit spoke to me and said, *It means more to give when you give all you have,* in relation to my not wanting to part with twenty dollars to give to Phyllis.

In that moment, the Holy Spirit tenderly chastised me and I inwardly wept and repented of my terrible thoughts and feelings. I was immediately ashamed of my feelings of superiority and convicted for the thoughts that I had been so self-righteous in my own giving.

Not only did I weep for the shameful feelings but I was also shown that, although I did tithe a substantial amount of the income that God blessed me with in the first place, I only gave what I felt I was supposed to, ten percent. But I had cheated God even in this, because my giving was ten percent of my net income, not my gross income. Rarely had I given even a penny more, and this church member was probably giving all she had from her very limited resources.

The Holy Spirit in His infinite mercy gently showed me through witnessing her selfless offering that I needed to be more generous of spirit. The monetary amount of an offering was not as important as was the spirit in which it was given. My tithing of a large offering was being degraded by the self-serving, superior spirit in which I had been giving it.

Every day is a challenge and I struggle to be the person He wants me to be. I am only human, so far from perfect, but through the love of Christ I can reflect, grow and attempt to learn from my mistakes and try not to repeat shameful actions. All along I thought I held myself to a higher standard and was shown through this instance how far I had yet to grow and learn from others. From that time forward whenever I find myself in a situation in which I feel superior to someone or something, the Holy Spirit quickens me to this consciousness, and I am forever grateful and strive to do better.

Thank You Father.

The Spirit Spoke

And how *is it that* we hear, each in our own language in which we were born? - Acts 2:8

It was one of our regular Sunday KRCC church services of worship and prayer. One youth in our church congregation was autistic and becoming a young man. In his development he was becoming more vocal throughout the service and becoming more of a handful for his mother to handle on her own as a single parent. His mom was devoted to Christ and devoted to her son and therefore faithful in bringing him to church regularly. The congregation became accustomed to his boisterous vocalizations.

After the service we would often congregate to chat, catch up and pray for one another. His mom asked some of the ladies to pray for him this particular Sunday. Soon a group of our senior church ladies were praying and laying hands on him, and I joined in. There was no space for me to actually lay hands on him, however, I laid hands one of my sisters who was touching him, and we continued to pray. I began to quietly pray in tongues, so as not to disturb the prayers that the other sisters were offering up to the Father for him. When the prayers ended, we gave thanks and we each went our way as the church service had been over before we began praying.

Getting ready to leave, I was waiting for Ed to finish packing up the worship instruments. Ed tithed his time through his service to the Lord and church by not only coordinating the set-up and take down of the weekly chairs and tables for the congregation seating area, he also set-up and tested the musical equipment, performed the drumming for the worship service and dismantled the equipment after the service. Of course, there were many congregational hands willing and able to help in these tasks, but Ed organized most of these activities to ensure everything ran smoothy each Sunday.

While waiting for Ed to finish his weekly tasks, I was standing quietly in the doorway leading to our reception area when unexpectedly and totally out of the blue, I felt strong arms hugging me from behind. The arms were so strong that I had to struggle to turn around in the grasp. It was the young autistic lad! I was beyond shocked! He was intently looking me directly in the eyes. His eyes were searching mine, and he was smiling and seemed to want to say something. However, being non-verbal he said nothing and after a few moments he let me go and walked away.

He had never previously acknowledged me or any of the other people in our church other than his mother that I was aware of, in any way before or since that one time. My only conclusion is that the Holy Spirit led him to understand the prayer I prayed in tongues. There remains no other plausible explanation for why he hugged me so intently that day, except the Holy Spirit spoke to him and this young man heard our Holy Father through my prayer in tongues. I saw this lad at church many times after this encounter, and he had never once acknowledged my presence in any way since that time.

I did not know what wondrous message the Father had for that young man that day, but I was humbled and blessed to be used by the Father to touch his spirit so profoundly; to be the conduit for this young man to hear supernaturally from his Father!.

To God be the glory!

Spiritual Impartation

Now Joshua the son of Nun was full of the spirit of wisdom, for Moses has laid his hands on him; so the children of Israel heeded him, and did as the Lord commanded Moses. - Deuteronomy 34:9

I experienced another remarkable release of the impartation of the Holy Spirit. One afternoon I had gone to visit a dear church sister who had extended an invitation for lunch. My sister was, and remains, a blessed and highly favoured child of God. She is highly respected and much loved throughout our church community and beyond for her passionate dedication to Christ. My sister is a consummate prayer warrior, faithful in prayer throughout her unwavering selfless service to others, on behalf of the Lord.

During our visit she prepared a light lunch, and after we had eaten, we were engaged in a time of prayer before I was to leave. During this time of prayer for our family members, our church, our community, and our government leaders we were holding hands. Then, something unusual happened. At the time when we had come to the end of the prayer, I was astonished to feel a flow of energy much like an electrical surge from me to my sister, through my hands to her hands. I felt her react to the sensation and I, too, was surprised by the feeling, but we did not speak of it to one another.

Not only was I surprised by the flow of energy, I was more surprised that it flowed from me to her, rather than from her to me. After all, I was the younger Christian and I revered her as a spiritual leader, mentor and aforementioned prayer warrior. This sensation led me to believe I had passed something to my sister that I was no longer in possession of, as if I had relinquished something. I had never experienced anything like this before.

Years later, I was still preoccupied by this unusual experience. It remained an unresolved anomaly that lingered in my mind. Attempting to make spiritual sense of this occurrence, I spoke with my spiritual sister Georgiana, who shared her insight. "We often believe we have nothing to offer, however I have learned even the strongest person at times needs to be strengthened, encouraged, and prayed for. In that moment of prayer, the Lord used you to do just that and that is what Christianity is all about, serving others." Her comments resonated with me and upon reflection of her insight, I believe God had taken from me His work that I was not worthy or equipped to undertake, and had given it to my dedicated sister for her willingness of service and her more-than-able spirit to perform. My dear church sister, with a willing heart to help others, was given a blessing to achieve, and fulfill more of the important community and spiritual service work of the Father, where I was woefully lacking.

Although Georgiana's comments put what happened in a better light for me, upon writing and sharing this experience I was encouraged to seek God. How could I reconcile this to God? I prayed for guidance and searched for scripture to uphold what I felt had transpired. Again, I do not profess to be holier than anyone else, certainly not my church sister whom I hold with in the highest regard, who had been serving the Lord for many years, long before I met her and was invited for lunch that day. But through prayer, God showed me biblically that He imparted wisdom to Joshua through Moses by the laying on of hands in Deuteronomy 34:9, quoted at the beginning of this account. I believe God chose to spiritually impart strength to my dear sister for her ministry work, on His behalf, which He had mightily planned out for her. I recognize I had nothing within me to strengthen my sister, I was simply the chosen vessel God used for His divine purpose. He had much more in store for her to do, in His service.

God will ensure that His wonderful plans will be fulfilled and will assign those who will be obedient to His Spirit in the things He asks. Just as He has assigned and is equipping my dear sister to perform her selfless service to others, I have been assigned to write this book of honour and praise to recognize His majesty!

Grace Sergeant

For by grace you have been saved through faith, and that not of yourselves; *it is* **the gift of God, not of works, lest anyone should boast. - Ephesians 2:8-9**

I missed my boy immensely and often played his "I Love You Mama" CD when I was alone riding in my car. I would think of his beautiful face and his unconditional and openly-proud love for me. One of my sweetest memories was when we were in the Pickering Town Centre one day. Michael was just beginning to reap solid recognition for his music in the industry; was performing at different venues and becoming well known in the area.

As we walked in the mall, we decided to part ways with a plan to meet up after our respective errands were complete. At the agreed-upon time, as I returned to the place we were to meet, I heard a commotion and saw a small crowd gathered. I thought to myself that there must be a celebrity making an appearance, as sometimes happened at the mall. As I got closer to the crowd, who did I see that was causing the stir but Michael! At six feet, four inches tall, he was head and shoulders above a group of squealing, adoring girls, clamouring around him. Michael had done a performance the weekend before, and one of the girls in the mall recognized him and was telling her friends all about it. Michael was obviously enjoying the attention. I stood back and watched this unfold before me, smiling and enjoying his attention almost as much as he was - proud mama after all.

Then Michael turned and saw me standing a short way off,

and I saw his face cloud over. He walked away from the girls and came directly over to me. He was serious as he put his arm around me and scolded: "Mom, don't you ever take a back seat to anyone. You are the most important person in my life, and you never stand aside for anyone where I am concerned!" I was surprised by his outburst but understood this came from his heart. Before I could respond, I realized the young girls had followed him and overheard him, and now their attention was turned to me. In their eyes I was immediately relegated to a higher status because I was his mom. I inwardly laughed to myself and Michael enjoyed this attention, deflected to me. We left the mall, his arm around my shoulder, with me teasing him about his new-found, star status. He had enjoyed the attention and I had enjoyed witnessing this new celebrity of his. It was a happy experience we shared together.

I would sometimes think back on this and many other wonderful memories when I listened to his CD. It dawned on me one day as I listened to his song that I would get a vanity license plate to commemorate his music. Michael had a tagline in his music, and I was excited as I decided that I would go and get vanity license plates that would remind me of him and his music. The day I went to order the vanity plates I was so excited because I had decided to use the tagline that he used in all his music, including the CD he made for me.

As usual there was a very long line when I got to the Ministry of Transportation Office (MTO). As I stood in line, I was in a quandary of how to spell his tagline and decided it must be "AHAA AHAA". The problem was there are only eight characters allowed on the plates, which would not allow for a space between the words, so I decided I would have to forego the space. The line for service was moving along and it finally became my turn. Surprisingly, the clerk, whom I didn't recognize, knew me from my work at the college where she said she had also worked for a short period of time. We exchanged pleasantries and I gave her my completed forms to obtain the vanity plate but felt something wasn't quite right, I didn't like

"AHAAAHAA". I went ahead and paid anyhow. I left the office and was on my way to the car, it came to me - it must read "AHA AHA". I knew this was the right way it should read and turned back to the motor vehicle office. The line was just as long as it had been originally with new patrons lining up, but I got in line anyway, anxious to make the change in the spelling.

As I waited in line, I filled out the new form for the revised spelling. I wondered whether I would have to pay again; the way some databases work I wondered if I would have to wait for the first spelling to clear their database before I could change it. A few things were running through my mind. When my turn finally came again, and I got up to the counter as luck would have it, I got the same clerk as I had the first time. Surprised to see me back, she asked how she could help me. I explained my dilemma; I had spelled the vanity plate incorrectly and needed to revise it. She was very helpful and told me that she could make the revision for me and I would not be charged to make the revision because it hadn't yet gone through.

I was so relieved as I submitted the new forms. I left the office happy that I would have a license plate that connected me with my boy. As time progressed, I was eager for the plate to arrive. It seemed to take forever, but it eventually arrived in February 2011. I gladly returned to MTO to register it and get a new sticker. I was beyond elated.

For six years, until 2017, I happily enjoyed my "AHA AHA" license plate. It's hard to explain the connection I felt to Michael every time I approached my car. It was as if he and I were driving together again in some special way. I was contented and it was comforting to me.

Then one day as I was reading my Bible I came across "aha aha" in the Bible. My heart felt like it had stopped. **They also opened their mouth wide against me,** *And* **said "Aha aha! Our eyes have seen it." - Psalm 35:21.** I didn't fully understand, but I knew the scripture was negative against the psalmist David and mocking him. Who would have thought "aha aha" would be in the Bible? I stifled my anxiety and chose to ignore the scripture. A few days later, I was reading on and found **"Let them be confounded because of their shame, Who say to me, "Aha aha!" - Psalm 40:15.** I was beside myself now; here it was again recorded in the Bible, the psalmist seeking confusion for those who mocked him. I was beyond understanding why I was finding this phrase in the Bible. I called my niece Teesha, who had a special connection with Michael, to tell her I found this reference in the Bible, in the hope she could help me understand, but we could not figure it out.

During the time I was finding these Bible scriptures, I had an occasion when I had stopped in the plaza, close to my home, to pick up some food for supper. Only expecting to be a moment, I parked illegally and I went inside the restaurant. When I came out, a parking officer was coming up the walkway close to where I was parked, he often patrolled the plaza giving out tickets. But, I had made it in time, and as I jumped into my car, he said to me in a disparaging way, "Ha ha ha," in response to seeing my license plate. He was obviously annoyed that I had parked where I had and, I supposed, because he didn't get to write me the ticket. I can't explain why, but I wanted to get out of my car and explain the plate to him, it wasn't meant to mock him or anyone else, it wasn't 'ha ha ha', it was "AHA AHA" and was meant to celebrate my son. But it was such a long story to get into with a perfect stranger, so I simply drove away feeling bad that he didn't understand the meaning of the plate. At the time, I didn't associate this incident with the mocking I found in the scripture, but the revelation came to me when I was writing this account. I realize this interaction may have been instigated by the Holy Spirit attempting to prompt me to understand the license plates had to be changed; since I had ignored the scripture references, I was being mocked!

Time progressed and I was being convicted in my spirit now because I knew the phrase was negative in its biblical context. And every day it was getting more and more evident in my spirit that I had to change the license plates. Every time I got into my car, instead of joy and a feeling of connection for Michael, I felt convicted to replace the vanity plates, even though I did not want to. I continued to put the scriptures in the back of my mind and attempted to justify to myself the plates on my car. I tried to reason with the Holy Spirit who relentlessly convicted me to change the plates, *Michael was my boy and this was my connection with him.*

It wasn't long before my Bible reading brought me to **Let them be turned back because of their shame, Who say "Aha aha!" - Psalm 70-3** This is the third time I found "aha aha" in the Bible! The psalmist was seeking relief from his adversaries. I asked myself, *How did this relate to Michael, his life, his innocence, his murderers, did it relate to his death somehow? Was there a message for me?*

It was then, and still is, too much for me to contemplate in my mind and in my spirit if this was a message of some kind. But I came to realize that, on its own, "aha aha" was wickedly spoken; referring to malicious laughter, mocking and derisive. A phrase that I thought brought Michael and I together, was biblically distressing. I didn't want to think of it, I didn't want to think anything negative concerning my boy or come to the realization I had to change my plates. I thought by having these plates, I was *honouring* him and his music. I didn't want to think about changing them.

By this time, almost six years had passed since I changed my plates to "AHA AHA," and they had brought me so much inner joy and peace. But after finding the phrase three times in the Bible and contemplating the meaning, I knew the time had come that I had to replace them. I struggled internally with making that decision. I spoke to Ed about it and he felt I was being too rigid in my thinking, and that the plates were fine. I also spoke to my daughter Sarah about it and she felt it was okay to leave them because she had felt all along that Michael's musical tagline was "uhuh uhuh." Even though they both supported the plates to stay as they were, it didn't make me feel any better. In my heart I was convicted to change the plate.

I truly struggled in my spirit and this was another extremely hard act of obedience I had to undertake, like not wanting to confess my lie to Ed and Sarah after I was baptized. I didn't want to change my plates; for me it was like I was abandoning my relationship with Michael. We spent so many good times in the car, driving back and forth to high school, then college and work. We spent those hours talking and sharing and forging our mother-son relationship. Thinking back, I am not surprised by the level of inner struggle I underwent. I expect a psychologist would say that, in my mind, I was in a way losing Michael again. I questioned why I had found those scriptures and I wondered if the phrase had any specific meaning for my son. I questioned why God was being so hard on me; He knew the significance those plates held in my heart. I was mad. I was angry that I was being convicted, but my resolve to obedience finally took precedence.

Despondent and with a sad heart, I set off to change my vanity plates. With my decision to change the plates I wanted to - no I *needed* to - acknowledge God in my act of obedience so I decided to change my plates to "HIS GRACE." Only God meant more to me than Michael; only for God would I change my plates.

When I got to the MTO, however, and tried to hand in the forms, I found, "HIS GRACE" was already assigned. I then asked the clerk if I could change them to simply "GRACE" instead. That too was taken. I was disheartened. At that moment I had another inner struggle with God. Here I was, attempting to be obedient in changing my plates and attempting to acknowledge His hand in my decision, yet I was being denied my choices and my attempts to do it. Something I didn't even want to do in the first place!

As I pondered what I was going to do to change the plates, the clerk suggested that I use my initials and place them before "GRACE," as in "SG GRACE," but my spirit shuddered at the suggestion because I knew I could not, in essence, place myself before grace, even on a license plate. I settled instead on "GRACE SG" and left the office.

As I had previously eagerly awaited the "AHA AHA" plates, I now hoped with the same fervour the new "GRACE SG" plates would take as long as possible to arrive, but they eventually came in September 2017. With a heavy heart I went again to motor vehicle to obtain the new sticker for the new plate.

I was unhappy. Although I felt I had done the right thing, I didn't like the new plates. I tried to like them; after all, the change was meant to recognize the Father's unfailing grace in my life. But honestly, I resented that I felt compelled in my spirit to change it. I asked God, *Wasn't it enough that I lost my son? Why did I have to lose the plates that reminded me of him as well?* I was rather petulant, like a child being told to do something they didn't want to do.

I drove my car with the new plate for a few months, then the Lord in His glorious way showed me He was pleased with my act of obedience. It happened when I had to go to my regular mechanic shop, Active Green + Ross, for my scheduled oil change. I left my car in the garage parking lot and went inside the office to make the arrangements. There was someone already in line ahead of me and the staff, who know me by name, said they would be with me momentarily. When it was my turn, I gave them my keys and told them I had new license plate to record on my file. I told them my new plate was "GRACE SG." Unbeknownst to me, a gentleman had entered the office behind me, and as I recited the new license plate to them, the gentleman behind me, said, "So *you're* the grace sergeant!" I was startled. I looked back at him and he smiled at me and repeated, "You're the grace sergeant!" I smiled back at him and simply said "Thank you, I had never thought of that." Immediately, I was spiritually uplifted.

I instantly knew God had orchestrated this gentleman's comment. To imagine that God could, and would, massage my heart in this way over the loss of my former plates was comforting and awesome in my spirit.

Since that brief encounter at the mechanic shop with a perfect stranger, I have proudly driven my car knowing that my act of obedience was in fact a response to an invitation from God to show my faithfulness to His desire in my life, even though I was resistant to comply. He had shown me He was well pleased by the act of surrendering my previous plates, especially in light of the sacrifice it was to my heart. And He restored my heart through my obedience. To think I might be perceived, by other drivers as a grace sargeant, an ambassador of Christ, is an honour I don't deserve, but a further indicator of Christ's grace toward me.

Bless You, Father.

He That is Within Me

You are of God little children, and have overcome them, because He who is in you is greater than he who is in the world. - 1 John 4:4

I was home alone. Ed had gone to visit one of his friends at the studio where he collaborated with some of Michael's young friends over music they were making. He had become a great mentor to these young men after Michael's passing. Sarah was out, I do not remember where she was particularly, maybe somewhere out with Jon.

Finding myself alone, I began praying and having a joyful worship time with the Lord. The house was otherwise quiet. Suddenly, I heard heavy footsteps moving around upstairs. Knowing I was alone in the house, I became frightened and my heart began to pound. Before I could move or make a sound, I heard those heavy footsteps move around more and begin to slowly descend down the stairs, one at a time. Terrified, in that split-second, I knew I was about to be faced with something otherworldly that I was beyond coping with. Instinctively in my mind I screamed out in defiance, *He that is within me, is greater than he that is in the world!*

Instantly I was saved from whatever the pending horror would have been. Whatever had been coming down the stairs was stopped in its tracks and came no further. I discerned the footsteps to be an act of the enemy, incensed that I was praising and worshiping God; there to scare me and stop me from doing so, but God's word stopped him from stopping me.

I was immediately relieved and felt the power of God's word wash over me and save me - from what, I thankfully did not see nor encounter! I continued in my worship, thankful to God for His blessing of protection and by His word, being covered in His blood, in the face of the enemy.

How Great Thou Art

Praise Him, all His angels; Praise Him, all His hosts! - Psalm 148:2

I was never so sweetly blessed, as another day, I was alone praising the Lord, and singing in worship to Him. As I told you, my heart's desire was to sing like my mother in all her gifted glory. Although this was not to be, the Father gifted me the desire to sing anyway. I was rewarded in my feeble attempts to sing and offer praise, when I heard an angel sing along with me this day.

In the midst of my worship, as I sang the legendary hymn, "How Great Thou Art," when I reached the chorus, I heard a small childlike voice singing along with me! This voice came from my left about three feet off the floor, and it was so heavenly inspired. The sweet voice was crystal clear and as melodious to my ears as wind chimes in the wind. At first, I thought I had imagined hearing it, and continued singing. I sang the second verse, and when I started to sing the chorus, again I heard the voice singing along with me. I believed I was being accompanied by an angel, and after I sang the third and fourth verses, I heard the angel continue to sing with me on the choruses.

When I came to the end of this glorious hymn, I thanked God for His divine favour and for sending an angel to sing with me. I knew the miracle I was receiving and wanted God and the angel to know I acknowledged His power and grace by so blessing me. Not long after this experience, I purchased wind chimes and set them outside my kitchen on our deck and I am daily and forever reminded of the sweet sound of the voice of the angel.

How blessed I have been throughout my lifetime by God's assignment of angels to be with and watch over me. I can testify that; I felt them as they lifted and kept me from falling when I tripped on the stairs during my sister Paula's wake, God made His angels known and showed them to me as they crowded my wall when Michael died, and now I was blessed to hear one sing with me. I bear witness, through God's divine impartation of heavenly gifts to me, *we are not alone!*

To God be the glory, for His mercy and favour on me, His unworthy servant.

God's Perfect Timing

He has made everything beautiful in its time. Also He has put eternity in their hearts, except that no one can find out the work that God does from beginning to end. - Ecclesiastes 3:11

Shortly after Michael died, I found two strings with wooden "Jesus" fish affixed to them, left on the doorknob on our front door. A young neighbor child who knew Michael had left them for Ed and I in condolence for our loss. To this day I have one hanging on my rearview mirror and remember the caring of this young lady I have yet to meet. How do I know it was a young lady? They say the apple doesn't fall far from the tree, and shortly after finding the fish, I met her mother, Nito. Through speaking with Nito, I discovered that it was her daughter who had left the Jesus fish on the doorknob.

Nito and I have forged a special spiritual bond destined through Christ our King. She has the most beautiful outward countenance, and the more I got to know her, I came to learn her outward beauty was only a small reflection of the beauty contained within her soul.

Our first encounter was at our neighbourhood community mail box when she offered her heart-felt condolences for our loss of Michael. I further learned that Michael had spent time a fair amount of time at her house as he was friends with her sons and her daughter. They lived 5 doors from us, but I had not met her previously, nor did I know that Michael spent time with her family. Her heart was grieved in her loss of my son, as much as for my loss, and she encouraged me to lean on Christ.

Over a number of years, we would occasionally meet at the mailbox or would see one another because I had to pass her house when I was returning home from work or errands. Because her house was across the street from the mailbox, we would often stop and have a wee chat. It became immediately evident that we shared a love of Christ, and we would speak and share our love of Him in our lives. I enjoyed speaking with her as I always felt a sense of warmth, comfort, quiet strength and love emanating from her. Nito surely was a special child of God.

Time passed, and one day I realized I hadn't seen her in a while, at least for a couple of months. At first, it was more a curiosity than anything, but as time continued to pass, I began to wonder where she was. I was even curious within my own mind and thoughts to why I was becoming so preoccupied with her absence? We hadn't visited each another's homes, although we often spoke of having a cup of tea together, so I didn't understand why Nito was so strongly on my mind throughout this time. I even considered going to knock on her door to inquire about her, but I did not follow through.

Busy at work one morning an immediate sense of urgency came over me regarding her. *Go get Nito flowers,* I heard the voice clearly say to me. I thought, *This is unbelievable.* It was so unexpected, out of the blue, but I couldn't shake the prompting. I tried to concentrate on my work and again I heard, *Go get Nito flowers.* The prompting persisted so much and was so strong that I decided to leave work in the middle of the morning to drive to a flower shop nearby. I exercised what my daughter liked to refer to as, "executive privilege" because as an Associate Registrar by this time, I enjoyed the opportunity to leave my desk without seeking permission, providing I made up any time missed. I simply told my staff I had to run an errand and would be back shortly. My plan was that I would go get the flowers, leave them in my car and drop them off to Nito on my way home. At least, that was the plan.

As I drove to the florist, a sense of internal urgency was building. When I arrived at the flower shop, I got one of those little cards and wrote a note to Nito saying that the flowers were a gift from God and that she was blessed and highly favoured. When I got back into my car with the flowers to return to work, the voice was there, *Go now, take the flowers now!* I again thought to myself, *This is bizarre.* Although I had a certain window of executive privilege, I argued with myself that I couldn't go the all the way home and then return back to work. I lived two towns over and it would take me at least an hour to go to Nito's and get back to work. But the voice persisted, actually rushing me, *Go, go now, take them now!* Knowing from previous experiences this was the Holy Spirit speaking to me, I replied aloud, "Okay, I'll go now." I called work and told my staff I would be delayed but would get back as soon as I could, and I headed to the highway.

I was prompted all along the way to Nito's house by the anxious command, *Hurry, hurry!* Finally arriving at her home, I got out of the car and retrieved the flowers from my back seat. As I approached her front door, I noticed there were new wood planks leaning against the side of the house, as though they were having some carpentry work done. I rang the bell - no answer. I rang the bell again, and again I got no answer. I now began to doubt the voice I heard. I spoke to God in my mind and asked why was I hurried and challenged to rush when there was no one home?

I found myself disappointed. I was anticipating Nito's happy reaction to receiving the flowers I had brought for her and tell her

But God, I Don't Want to Write a Book!

how God had prompted the gift. But no one answered the door and I began to think this was all my idea and I hadn't been prompted by the Spirit at all. I felt a bit foolish, but I had the flowers and I decided to leave them anyway. I was concerned however, that a passerby might see them sitting on the doorstep and take them before someone got home. So, I placed them just behind the wooden planks in such a way that they would be noticed by someone coming home, but would not be visible from the front of the street.

I left to return back to work, totally cast down that I had just gone through all this, seemingly on my own accord, not because I was prompted by God. I had experienced so many past instances of hearing and following the prompting of the Spirit, I had been sure I was following the same prompting in this situation too.

That evening my doorbell rang. I fully expected Nito would be coming to thank me for the flowers and so it was, Nito at the door. I told her straight away that the flowers were not from me, but that God had prompted me to leave work, go get the flowers and deliver them to her. She listened quietly, then she shared with me that on her own time she had been counselling the mother of one of her sons' friends, who was experiencing some terrible upheaval in her life. She explained she had spent more time, and more evenings, than she initially expected she would, but felt compelled to support this woman who so desperately needed her help. She said her counselling of this lady was taking a physical toll, and she said she was tired and not sure how much she was actually helping her. She went on to say, when she got home earlier that evening, her son said she had flowers. She got the flowers and the note that I had left, that said the flowers were a gift from God.

She thanked me and said she knew the flowers were sent by God. As Nito was relaying her story, she could hardly get the words out. After she told me of how tired she was in counselling this lady, all the time she had committed, and more importantly, how she was questioning whether she was making an impact, she said she knew the flowers were from God by His confirmation. I wondered how did she know? Nito had tears in her eyes as she shared with me His holy confirmation - the name of the person she had been counselling was *Sherry*! That the lady who Nito was helping, and I sharing the same name, was His confirmation to her that He had seen and awarded her sacrifice, by having me bring her the flowers. Further evidence that *there are no coincidences in Christ*!

I am amazed how our blessed Father choreographs His desires for us. For months the Lord had set me on this path to make His blessing come to fruition, for such a perfect time as this, on behalf of His faithful daughter, Nito. He quickened her to my thoughts over a period of months and then, just when it was His appointed time for her to receive her reward, He hastened my spirit to act at the precise time of His choosing. I again thank the Lord for my spirit of obedience which always, *without fail* leads to His joyful blessings of others and at the same time, for me.

Upon reflection I know that it was not by accident, but by His marvelous design, that no one was home to receive the flowers. I believe it was God's plan for me to leave them for her. Had someone been home, the gift of flowers would have been about me giving the flowers and not about God's reward. All this was orchestrated by His wonderful and wondrous divine power.

This is such a magnificent reflection of how God will use those who will listen and be obedient to his prompting of His Spirit to do His work. Nito, in her service of helping this lady, became the recipient of God's blessing through the flowers. We both believe and recognize that God in His mercy and grace had openly rewarded Nito's selfless sacrifice through her own commitment in her service to Sherry. His generous act of love toward her, divinely encouraged her to continue her service to Sherry who needed her. And God used me as His special flower deliverer, I am eternally blessed to be part of His magnificent plans.

We serve a most glorious God!

Flowers Flourished

Declare His glory among the nations, His wonders among all peoples. - Psalm 96:3

Just as the Father gifted my special friend Nito with flowers, I want to share with you another incredible experience involving flowers. I had received a birthday gift of flowers from a dear friend and colleague Terry. Terry and I forged a strong relationship through our financial aid leadership roles within the Ontario Association of Student Financial Aid Officers, OASFAA. Our professional relationship blossomed into a strong personal kinship that I cherish today. Terry and I could not be more dissimilar in our physical appearances, but we are tied together by a spirit of love and purpose that could only be ordained by God.

Being a recipient of flowers on only a few occasions, I appreciated her generous birthday gift to me. As I took them out of their packaging and prepared a vase to set them in, a thought crossed my mind to share them. Once I had them ready for display, I took them into my dining room which also serves as my prayer room. In this sanctuary, I made room on my table for my Bible so I could do my scripture readings, and have a place to pray and sing my worship songs every day. This was also the room where I had witnessed the multitude of angels on the wall after my son had died, and the place where I heard the angel singing with me. It was in this room I chose to thank the angels, by sharing my flowers with them.

As I entered the room, I set the flowers on the table. I spoke aloud to the angels that I know surround us. I acknowledged their presence and thanked them for lighting my path and guiding my way. I told them I wanted to share the flowers with them to enjoy, and I set the flowers on the table.

After about a week, I realized the flowers were still thriving, when they should certainly have begun to fade and die. Instead of dying, the flowers appeared to be getting brighter and brighter, and a sweet aroma filled the dining-room. I continued to refresh the water they were placed in, but it soon became evident there was more at work than my simple watering that was keeping these flowers fresh. This went on for more than a month; it would have been unbelievable if I had not already experienced the many amazing works of God and His angels in my life.

Speaking to the angels again, I told them I recognized the flowers were thriving when they should not have been. I said I hoped they were enjoying them. Soon after this declaration, the flowers did slowly begin to fade. I felt that the angels appreciated my acknowledgement of them, not only through my sharing of the flowers, but by the inexplicable prolonged life of those flowers to recognize their presence.

I am left to wonder if the angels had any power to prolong the life of the flowers themselves, or if not by their own actions, I ask myself could it have been our heavenly Father. Could He have wanted to honour their service to me, much like He did to honour Nito for her compassionate service.

Only God knows.

Welcome Home

Now faith is the substance of things hoped for, the evidence of things not seen. - Hebrews 11:1

My daughter Sarah and son-in-law Jon were married as I previously shared on October 10, 2014. The agreed-upon-plan was that, when they returned from their honeymoon in Florida, they would return to live with Ed and I. They would live with us for a couple of years in order to establish themselves financially and prepare for their future. We were happy to have them reside with us and we looked forward to their return and starting their married life together.

While they were away, Ed and I decided we would prepare Michael's bedroom for them. Sarah had her own bedroom at the time, but Michael's bedroom was bigger, and we felt it was time that we opened his room for the living. We had kept it the same way it was, since he died in 2007, and we felt there was no better way to welcome Jon into our family and our home. Michael could never be replaced in our hearts, but in some way by allowing them to have his room, it would not only recognize the son the Lord gave us, but acknowledge the son we would gain by welcoming Jon into our family.

We had a lot of work to do in preparation for their return. Michael had all the walls from end to end plastered with a variety of pictures; he had items hanging from the ceiling illustrating brand names and special purchases. He collected baseball caps, and all of them they were positioned and hung on the walls over the pictures. In addition to removing all these items from the walls, we had to pack up all his clothes out of his closet and empty all his dresser drawers. Through the mechanics of doing all this, our hearts were in conflict for deciding, in essence, to move on from Michael's room being Michael's room to letting Sarah and Jon move in to start their life. We felt sad that we were letting Michael go in a sense. But we had discussed it at great length before we made the decision, and we felt Michael would approve. That is the only thing that gave us the strength to proceed.

After packing up Michael's possessions we purchased new bedding and a colourful banner that read "Welcome Home." We cleaned the room for Sarah and Jon's arrival and the day they were due to arrive back, I made up the bed with the new bedding and Ed and I installed the banner across the room so they would see it as soon as they opened the bedroom door. Finally, we were finished cleaning and preparing the room. We were finally ready and looking forward to their pending arrival, later that day.

As the day wore on, I went back into the bedroom one more time to view our handiwork only to find a big bum print outlined in the new bedding on the side of the bed. I straightened out the cover on the bed, closed the door behind me and went back downstairs. In passing, I said to Ed he should have fixed the bed after sitting on it because he left his bum print on the side of the bed. After a brief back-and-forth conversation to determine what I was talking about, Ed assured me he had not sat on the bed when we were in there, and more pointedly, he had not been in the room since we had left the room together earlier.

I am left to wonder where the bum print came from. In my heart of hearts, I believe Michael had returned to his room one last time and sat down while he pondered this new development; wanting to spend some time in there one final time. I have faith he understands the endless love we all have for him, but there is a small part of my heart that wonders if he may have felt sad, as Ed and I had, that his room was no longer going to be considered his. We take comfort in knowing that Michael dearly loved his sister, and would wish her well on the new marriage journey on which she was embarking. He could also keep an eye on her.

We love you Michael.

Michael's Last Visit

And God will wipe away every tear from their eyes, there shall be no more death, nor sorrow, nor crying. There shall be no more pain, for the former things have passed away. - Revelation 21:4

Ed had a series of three knee surgeries during the winter of 2017-18. After what was supposed to be a routine knee replacement, he suffered a setback that resulted in the new knee shifting out of place. He had to undergo the second operation to redo the original knee replacement. The third operation was performed as an emergency, after a regularly scheduled doctor checkup, when it was determined a hole in his leg was necrosis and needed immediate attention and action. We had to rush him to the hospital the same day for this third operation.

When we arrived at the hospital to have the necrosis attended to, Ed was admitted and sedated. It was then the surgeon came out and told me there was a chance that Ed could lose his leg and worse still, even his life. Because Ed was already under sedation, I had to give consent and sign the papers in the event, once the doctor got in to assess the damage, he could proceed without further delay if he had to amputate Ed's leg. My only choice was to sign the papers with a heavy heart so the doctor could do what he had to do if necessary. After I signed the papers, I immediately called Ed's sister, Sandra, in Boston so she could apprise their family of this dreadful turn of events. I went to the hospital prayer room and extended fervent prayers for my husband because I did not want him to lose his life or his leg. It would be a horror for him to wake up to find his leg gone. How could I ever explain to him I had to sign the papers? I refused to let my mind go to the worse-case scenario, that he would not survive.

Through the grace of our Lord Most High, Ed survived the operation with this leg intact, but he had a long road of recovery ahead. Eventually, he was on his way to healing. Through a combination of his internal fortitude, personal support workers, physiotherapists, doctor visits and my devotion to his daily exercise regime, he was soon on the mend. It was, however, a harrowing time, and we continually give thanks that God spared his life and his leg.

It was during Ed's recuperation period when I last saw Michael's spirit. When Michael was alive, he was adamant that I would not have to shovel snow in the winter, or mow the lawn in the summer, and I was happy to let him and his dad take care of those duties. But during the winter, while Ed was convalescing from the three back-to-back knee surgeries, he was not able, nor permitted, to shovel. He is a proud man and did not enjoy that I had to do this work. Fortunately, I did have the help of my son-in-law Jonathon; our lovely neighbours Denise and Eric who lived next door; and one neighbor Tom, who lived across the street, who often came over to help whenever he saw me outside shovelling alone.

As luck would have it, one day it snowed and there was no one around to help. Jon was still at work and I didn't see any of the neighbours. I didn't want the snow to pile up, so instead of waiting for Jon to come home or any the neighbours to come out, I decided to start shovelling.

When I got about half way through shovelling the driveway, I stopped to take a break and looked up. That is when I saw his spirit. Michael was standing in the front corner of the garage watching me shovel! It was only a fleeting moment, but he had on a pair of tan pants that he often wore and I particularly liked. I smiled to myself because I knew he was watching out for me and probably, by his presence, trying to remind me he didn't like to see me shovel. When I finished and went back into the house, I told Ed that I had seen Michael watching me. Ed came to the same conclusion I had - that Michael was watching and didn't like it that I was shovelling.

I was comforted by Michael's presence because l wanted to believe that he watched over our family while Ed continued to recuperate, and this gave me a great sense of comfort.

That was my last known visit from my beautiful boy.

CHAPTER 9

God's Favour

For the gifts and calling of God *are* irrevocable. - Romans 11:29

There have been so many extraordinary experiences and relationships borne of God in my life, as I have shared. He, in all His glory and for His purpose, has elected that I have a special place in the hearts of others. God has shown me favour in the eyes of so many and His grace has followed me throughout my life's journey. I have been given so much love through so many remarkable relationships and gifts, that I can't even begin to list or acknowledge them all here. Each and every one is cherished and has a place of honour in my heart.

Many spiritual and heavenly gifts I have already shared with you. Some earthly gifts I would also like to share with you so as to shine a light on the impartation of God's mercy, grace and loving-kindness toward me and how He has woven these special gifts in my life.

My younger sister Lynn wrote me a heart-felt letter to remind me how blessed I was to have been Michael's mother, ending with a divine impartation of God's word. With Lynn's permission, I include her letter for you here.

SCHERRY,

Your Beautiful, Beautiful Baby. Your Beautiful Son, Michael. GOD entrusted Only 'you' to take care of this 'Special Child'. To Love and to Nurture for 25 Wonderful Years. Michael was everything that you could ask for in a son. 'You' are the one GOD blessed to raise him up and to fulfill each other with Joy and Happiness. I know Michael was your 'Pride and Joy', and there will be no other like 'him'.

No one could have Blessed you in the Special Way that Michael did. So pure of heart, so innocent, so loving, so kind, so full of joy, so much of you. So Blessed to be of you. You so blessed to be of him.

His physical, was his vessel and I know you (we) will miss him fiercely, but his real identity is his spirit, which is now with JESUS, in Michael's eternal home. Now, Safe and Sound. Now, no more Tears. Now, no more Pain. Now, no more Sorrow or Grief. Just 'GLORY AND LOVE', FOREVER.

When we are reunited, we will be joined together again, NEVER to be SEPARATED again. Our Family together, always in 'Love and Peace'.

BLESSED are you Scherry, who was Loaned this 'Special Being".

BLESSED are you Scherry, from the Love you Shared.

BLESSED are you Scherry, for the 'Impartation' that you blessed Michael with.

BLESSED are you Scherry, for the 25 Years of 'UNCONDITIONAL LOVE'.

BLESSED are Ed and Sarah (Princess) that they shared in this 'Union'.

The 'Sweet, Sweet' Aroma of Michael's life will be with you Always. The 'Fragrance of His Love' will whisper in your ear. The 'Depth of the Love' will be breathed into Your very Being, Daily.

Your 'Michael' was stolen from you, but GOD in HIS 'Tender Mercies', lifted Michael up into HIS HANDS and Gathered him unto 'HIMSELF'

Love and Sorrow

Your Sister Lynn

SCHERRY;

THE LOVE THAT YOU AND MICHAEL SHARED, WAS NOT OF THIS WORLD, IT WAS IMPARTED FROM ME. MY WAY OF LOVE, AN EVERLASTING LOVE. I AM VERY PLEASED WITH THE LOVE (MICHAEL) THAT I TRUSTED YOU WITH. I WILL CARRY YOU IN YOUR SORROW AND I WILL CARRY YOU THROUGH YOUR PAIN. I WILL NEVER LEAVE OR FORSAKE YOU. LEAN ON ME BECAUSE I AM YOUR

STRENGTH. MY LOVE WILL SUSTAIN YOU AND YOUR FAMILY. MICHAEL IS WITH ME NOW AND I THANK YOU FOR OUR LOVE THAT YOU GAVE HIM.

MASTER AND SAVIOUR

JESUS CHRIST

…………..

My oldest daughter Chantal wrote an original poem commemorating her love for her baby brother, Blue. With Chantal's permission I would like to share the poem she wrote and recited to the congregation, during Michael's funeral:

My Friend, My Hero, My Baby Brother Blue

I put this pen to paper with both sadness with and joy,
The gentle man we mourn today began a gentle boy.
My brother Michael, Tricksta, Blue, was everybody's friend
He always had an encouraging word or a helping hand to lend.

It's with a smile that I recall my brother's hearty laugh.
He always strove to do his best, not satisfied with half.
Those of us who knew him well, know his shoes got special care.
I hope that where he is right now, he has a million pair.

Each one of us will take away unique memories of him.
He touched us all so personally that those
special thoughts won't dim.
The adoration he received, he gave back a hundred-fold,
And through his spirit, words and music,
we're left with much to hold.

His integrity was flawless, and cheerfulness, uplifting
His loyalty could not be matched, his morals never shifting.
We all know that his word was gold, he was not a pretender.
Perhaps if there'd been a search for saints,
he'd've made an apt contender.

The essence that was Michael George
transcends these earthly words
Our speech cannot explain and so our sentiments must be heard.
He gave a special something to every family member and friend
We all can feel it in our hearts, to a depth that doesn't end.
'To know him was to love him', is a phrase that's used a lot
If a picture went along with it, his face would fill that spot.
Protective, loving, funny, generous – a better
brother you could not design.
I'm proud and oh so fortunate that I had him as mine.

Thank you.
Written with love by Chantal Danise on August 2, 2007

....

Many people, in addition to family, shared gifts with me. One such gift I must share with you because of the deep impact it engraved on my heart. Tatiana, a former staff member, sent me a small figurine of a woman cradling a baby, and every time I look at it, my heart is filled with remembrance and love for Michael. This was the first gift I received after Michael died and I cherish this mother-child representation of love deep in my heart. God has imprinted love in my spirit for him as a baby through this figurine which is warm and comforting, and I am so thankful. I doubt that Tatiana understood the significance this loving gesture would have in my life since Michael has been gone, but I am forever grateful to her for her wonderful expression. Every morning and every night, as

I say my first and final prayers and give thanks to God for Michael, I look upon this expression of love and am deeply comforted.

God also enlisted those I didn't even know to shower me with blessings. A young man, who I only know by his initials, "AR," because that is all I can read on his painted portrait of Michael. This talented young man saw Michael's obituary in the paper that included a coloured picture. He didn't know Michael but was so moved by his death and by our family's loss, in his compassion, he painted a portrait of the picture that was in the obituary and presented it to us at an event we all attended. We still are no further ahead in finding the perpetrators of Michael's murder, but this portrait hangs proudly in our family room, a forever reminder of our wonderful son and a stranger's compassion.

I also received an especially poignant special portrait of Michael that shows him at three years old, a replica of a picture taken at his daycare many years ago. I was chastened with inner shame as I accepted this loving portrait. I felt a deep sense of guilt in my spirit for the generosity of the giver of this incredible gift. I had previously rejected a relationship with Frances, a painter and long-time friend of my father. We had experienced a disagreement, born out of my selfish desire to exclude her from my relationships, because she was a friend of my dad. Through my immature actions, she was hurt and we chose to tolerate one another at best following the disagreement. I could therefore not have been more surprised, ashamed or more humbled, when I received the portrait she had painted many years prior, when Michael was just a child. I hadn't even been aware she had painted Michael's picture before I received it from her. At his passing, she rose above my earlier pettiness and sent me this striking portrait of my son. The portrait hangs proudly in Michael's favourite room, the white room, above his urn; a constant reminder of his handsome, young self.

I wrote a long letter and reached out by phone to Frances and asked for her forgiveness for my previous actions, and thanked her for her kindness toward me. How does one reconcile the unmerited favour of others, especially when least deserved? Frances's actions mirrored the grace and loving-kindness of Christ that will be etched in my heart forever. Frances has since passed away, but I am so thankful in my heart for our coming together, born of her forgiveness and graciousness shown toward to me.

I have so many extraordinary memories. Quite unexpectedly at work one day, I was given an older period-painting of a young Black girl and boy. The girl is in a window combing her hair while looking out at the boy playing in the street. This gift from a colleague who seemed puzzled when she told me, that as she sat at her computer, she was unable to get the thought out of her mind that this painting that she had displayed on her office wall, should belong to my family, especially me! She felt that I would find comfort in it, and I certainly did. I thought at the time, her generosity was to remind me of Sarah and Michael playing as young children, and I thanked God for prompting her spirit. What was so puzzling and makes this so unusual is, that although Christine and I were colleagues and exchanged pleasantries whenever we saw each another, we were not what I would refer to as particularly close friends. That is what makes this so significant. She said she was *led* to give me the painting by a feeling, a voice, a pushing of the spirit. I believe God ordained her, in her spirit, to grant me this gift. Christine was obedient to the prompting of her spirit to give me the painting, and I marveled that she presented me with this sudden kindness.

A few days or so later, I couldn't contain my smile as Christine came to me again, with another painting. She told me that the paintings needed to be together. This second painting was the matching artwork by the same artist. This painting shows two Black women sewing in their parlour, obviously set in the same time period, as in the painting of the children. Christine said she was being urged by a feeling over a few days to, *Go bring it, go bring it,* so she, being obedient to the urging, was compelled to also give it to me.

I accepted these works of art that were given with love, devotion and through the prompting of the Spirit. Although Christine never expressed to me that God told her to give me these beautiful artworks, in my heart I know He authored her actions. Interestingly, the ladies in this painting look like my paternal relatives, my great-aunt Goldie and my aunt Donalda; may they both rest in peace. A precious benefit of these resemblances are the fond memories I am reminded of: the warm days of summer; the sound of country crickets and the birds, the smells and tastes of warm home-baked bread and the many love-filled hugs, when our family would drive and vacation in New Glasgow, Nova Scotia, to visit all our relatives who lived there.

So many hearts were generously opened up to me. I also received from an adorable colleague, Paolina, a diminutive fairy that reminds me of her petite stature. I graciously accepted a framed print of a "Buffalo Spirit," painted by a Cree artist, from a great thinker and orator, Anthony. God has blessed me beyond words.

It is not just the magnificent physical gifts I cherish; it is more notably the love with which they have been given to me, the impartation of God's favour toward me that I see interwoven, into each one.

More gifts continued to flow to me. I came to know Joan through her son, John who I worked with me at the college. Joan was from Newfoundland yet gained a reputation at the college through all the wonderful treats she would bake and give to John, when he visited with her, to share with his colleagues when he returned to Ontario. John and I shared a great relationship and I asked him one time if he would like to pray when he shared his mom was suffering a medical issue. Through our occasion of praying, John shared that Joan too, was God-fearing. Joan recovered from her illness, and she I became special friends through our mutual love of Christ. Joan continued to send her home-baked goods to me and others, and when she came to visit, John made sure that she and I met in person. We had an instant bond born of the spirit, and I regarded Joan with great love and affection.

The last time I saw Joan was during John's retirement party. Because I was one of the speakers, I incorporated her and her baking into the speech, which I hoped made her feel as special as she was regarded by everyone.

God called Joan home in 2019, and she left much love in my heart in her passing. John came to visit me after Joan had passed and gave me something to remember her. He and his wife, Trudy, thought that Joan would want me to have this reminder, a pin with two small hearts connected and intertwined. What a perfect reflection of the relationship that Joan and I shared.

Thank you, Father, for the friendship between Joan and I, inspired through our shared love of, and for, You.

Another particularly God-inspired gift was from a cherished colleague I worked with, a bit more closely on some occasions, than others. I shared my love of God with Malcolm, a faculty member on a number of occasions. Malcolm worked at a different campus but we saw each other as our work required. Malcolm and I shared a bond of the spirit from when we first met. Little did we know how God would translate our connection into yet another special gift that I will forever cherish.

At this particular time, I was experiencing some major medical challenges with the onset of carpal tunnel syndrome. The condition was deteriorating so badly that I could not properly hold the steering wheel when I was driving. Many nights were spent sleepless due to the pain that would travel up my wrist into my forearm. Texting and typing at work were almost unbearable, but the worst challenge I faced was losing the dexterity in my right hand. I loved to proudly wear my cross that Jenny had brought back to me from Greece some years prior, but I could no longer open and close the small clasp on the chain. Every day as I dressed for work, I would silently lament the fact that I could not wear my cross because I was unable to unfasten, or fasten it. I missed wearing my cross and felt saddened.

Malcolm came to see me one day. As I said, he taught at a different campus but had occasion to be at my campus, and he dropped by my office. We always had a great connection and conversations, and I was happy to have an opportunity to chat.

Malcolm sat down and said he had a present for me. He had recently taken a Journalism class he taught to Brazil, and while there had visited the Christ the Redeemer statue. He said that on a table in a market at the foot of the statue, he found something that he just *had to* purchase for me. Malcolm gave me a small box. When I opened it, it contained a cross - not just any cross. It was a small replica of Christ the Redeemer statue, and it was on a chain that went from one side of the cross to the other. It did not have a clasp on it. I could wear this cross by slipping it over my head!

How could this gift be anything but the work of Christ who, through Malcolm, gave me a cross to wear that did not require me to fasten a clasp! Even while I suffered with the carpal tunnel symptoms, this cross was easy to slip over my head. God supplied my need, and desire, to openly share my faith by giving me a cross that I could easily wear. How many times have I shared that *there are no coincidences in Christ?*.

Praise God for His tender mercies.

God Restored My Heart

And we know that all things work together for good to those who love God, to those who are the called according to *His* purpose. - Romans 8:28

God is merciful and didn't stop at earthly, physical gifts. He restored love in my heart by bringing people in my life who took it upon themselves to love me unconditionally.

One of my most cherished gifts was a relationship I shared with a remarkable lady who I liked to refer to as my "mom away from mom." Her name was Janet. Although my mom was alive during the time of Janet's and my relationship, and was very much a part of my life, my mom was many miles away and Janet assumed many characteristics of a loving mom to me. She baked me birthday cakes, gave me advice and provided a broad set of shoulders to lean on throughout many years. She was a source of strength when Michael died and when her beloved daughter Teri died years later, I would like to think I was a source of prayer and strength for her as well. Janet passed away in 2017, and in her passing she left behind a world of love and laughter, not only to me, but to all those who were fortunate to share this life with her.

As you now know, my son was stolen by dark forces roaming the earth to hate, destroy and kill. In his innocence he was taken for yet unknown earthly reasons. I have often felt that those who killed Michael better repent in this life, or, woe to them, they will have to pay in the next life, and it will be devastatingly sorrowful for them. God, in His loving-kindness, has allowed me to leave the murderers to Him, with that sentiment of their fate in my heart. They took Michael, but by God's tender mercies, I will not despair by allowing them to take away any more from me.

While God has permitted peace in my spirit, for reasons already shared, He has additionally done so, in part, by placing a young man who, for all intents and purposes, has personally, and by his own efforts, undertaken the role of a son in my life where Michael would have been. I am forever grateful that God ordained our relationship.

I met this young man under what could have been adverse conditions. A requirement of my financial aid job was such, that at the beginning of each semester, we were faced with long lineups of often frustrated students, attempting to secure their financial aid for the semester, that we had to accommodate. Tempers sometimes ran high, as government rules dictated processes, including the presentation of specific identification by students, seeking to obtain their financial aid; especially when a student arrived without the required identification, having already invested time in the lineup. My staff and I sometimes faced the unwarranted ire of these students. It was during one of these incidences I met Mede. He and his twin brother Aide, had arrived to the front of the line after a long wait, to pick up their financial aid. Mede had forgotten his identification in the car and was attempting to secure his assistance without presenting it. I happened to be stationed at the front of our financial aid operation checking identification, and he and his brother were not happy that I was not letting them go any further, without the required identification. I steeled myself for the usual arguments and occasional name calling as I reiterated the rules and told Mede he had to go out to his car and retrieve his identification before I could let him proceed.

I knew these young men were different, as shown by Aide's reaction. Expecting a barrage of profanities, or worse, he simply said to me, "Miss, you should have breakfast before you come to work in the morning." I smiled; I couldn't believe my ears. I was expecting to be called out of my name or have a loud raucous argument and this relatively mild comment is all I was met with. I knew there was something unique about these two young men and immediately thought that they must have had a wonderful upbringing if this was as harsh as they were going to get in their frustration. I came to find out later that Aide is a reverent and faithful son of God. Mede retrieved his identification, and we eventually concluded his business. They impressed me as respectful young men at a time when young Black men were thought to be rude, reckless and often worse.

Sometime later I was looking to hire a work-study student, and Mede and Aide came to mind. Aide was in his final semester, so I was not inclined to invest in training him, but Mede was in his first year, and therefore a better candidate. I often liked to hire those students who demonstrated or vocalized issues with our processes with the intent to educate them to the business side of our service. My staff did not always agree with this tactic, but I found some of my best staff as a result of giving opportunity where none previously existed. I imagined that Mede would flourish if given the opportunity. I was right.

Michael was attending the college at this time and working

as a work-study student in the gym. Shortly after he graduated, a temporary part-time position became available in the financial aid department and he was hired. He did not immediately report to me, so it was not an issue at the time, but eventually hiring protocols started to change. A full-time position became available that had to be posted to advertise for suitable applicants. Under the protocol for full-time employment, Michael would not be allowed to continue in my department because, although he had reported to my assistant, my assistant's position was not a managerial one, and technically that meant that Michael would report directly to me. He started to look for other positions at the college.

Michael and Mede, one year in age between them, became acquaintances; they also knew each other through their academics and their work in the financial aid office. They often met up in the same circles during their social activities, of which I had no knowledge at the time. However, on one occasion Michael came to me and said he had run into Mede over the weekend at an event. He said Mede had a few drinks and had approached him saying, "I don't care if you think I'm soft man, I love your mother." Michael got a big kick out of this; he knew it was a purely platonic comment, and he was amused yet thrilled, that Mede said he loved me straight out to him. Michael loved anyone who loved me.

During this time Mede had also been working part-time in my department when the full-time permanent position became available. He came to me feeling poorly because he felt he was "taking Michael's job." Mede had proven to be a great worker: he established good relationships with students, he was dependable and smart and he learned all the necessary requirements of the position. I told him it wasn't Michael's job and Michael couldn't be hired into the full-time position anyway. I encouraged him to apply. I said to him "Mede, if I can't have Michael, I wouldn't want anyone else but you."

Mede applied and was eventually hired permanently in my department. Michael did obtain another job at the college and was due to begin on Monday, July 30, 2007 but was killed in the early hours of Sunday, July 29, so he never got to start his new job. When Michael died, Mede adopted my family and especially me. He made himself available and took it upon himself to try to fill the void left in my heart.

I can't explain the depth of the bond Mede and I share, and I believe God had started His plan to join us together on that first day we met when he showed up without his identification. He and his brother were special even then. I can't help but reflect on the earlier conversation in which Mede would tell Michael he loved me and the conversation in which I would tell Mede, if I couldn't have Michael, then I didn't want anyone else but him. How little did any of us know how significant those seemingly innocent comments would become? In hindsight, I believe these conversations were forerunners of the relationship upon which we were about to embark that God had preordained.

Mede has been my steady rock. He cares for Sarah and Ed, as much as he cares for me. He remembers holidays, my birthdays, Mother's Day. All the things that Michael used to love to celebrate with me, Mede remembers. He has blessed me with many gifts from his heart and I want to acknowledge only a few: a large painting of a mother cradling her child, a stone lion for protection, a figurine of an African mother carrying her child on her back, a charcoal sketch of the Christ holding a lamb, and a plaque that reads, "Life is Hard, Stay Prayed Up." I have such love in my heart for his generosity of spirit towards me.

I have to thank Mede's family, especially his mother Ailene and his father Reku, for graciously and generously sharing this special young man, their son Mede, with me. I wish to acknowledge their blessing and to commend them on their beautiful three sons including Aide, Mede's twin, and their youngest, Reme, whom they have raised and nurtured into beautiful, upstanding, and respectful Black men.

Only God could have brought Mede to me. He has been a

constant in my life since Michael died. Through watching him mature in life, I can imagine how Michael would have continued to thrive and grow into manhood, had he not been taken away.

Just as God had given me the love and caring of a young man close in Michael's age in Mede, He also gave me another young man Ahmed, whom I also met through the college. Ahmed is a powerful man of God; an unreservedly proud Christian, a strong, Black, married father of five with deep love of family. I had the pleasure of watching him grow from student to father to business owner. He and I spent many occasions talking about our love of God, and he would share with me his vast knowledge of the Bible. Ahmed is a spiritually-gifted young man, and he taught me so much about the history in the Bible, things I didn't learn in church. We shared many deep spiritual conversations, and I told him of many of the experiences I am sharing in this book. Back then, I also told Ahmed I was supposed to write a book one day because God was telling me this was my task; I just wasn't sure when it was going to happen. Ahmed encouraged me and told me he would purchase the first copy when I did so. He continued over the years to remind me that I had to complete this task, and how he felt others may be blessed by what the Lord has given me to tell.

Ahmed and Mede were my greatest supporters during much of my latter years at the college, before I retired. We often prayed for, and with, one another in my office as issues surfaced in our lives. God did that. God provided opportunities for us to openly love Him and seek His face at His throne of grace, for anything or anyone at any time. God watched over us and guided our steps. God gave me these young men, not as a replacement for my son Michael, but that each of them would stand on their own, full of love from Christ, to me.

I wish to illustrate their special kindness in my life. Due to the COVID-19 pandemic, I could not have a proper retirement party in August 2020 so they, along with Mede's girlfriend, Sonia, came to my home carrying balloons and a cake to celebrate with me, respecting social distancing of the day. Mede and Ahmed, each wrote and presented to me heartfelt letters of their feelings regarding our relationships that brought tears to my eyes but so much joy to my heart. I could never repay or replace the love they've shown to me.

Most importantly, they presented me with a placard of love quoting scripture which I shared at the beginning of this segment; **And we know that all things work together for good to those who love God, to those who are the called according to *His* purpose - Romans 8:28.** It is significant that I repeat the scripture here because I am not sure they understood this scripture was intended for *them* all along, as much as they had thought it had been intended for me. *They were* "called according to His purpose," to be by my side all these years.

"I hereby thank You and acknowledge to You, Father God that Mede and Ahmed have done well in their task to which You called them, to walk beside me. By the obedience of their actions, I remain stronger, and I present these two young men to You as a request to be pleasing in Your sight. I ask favour for each of them in their lives, and in the lives of all those they hold dear, such as they have shown and given me. Amen."

My heart has been continually strengthened by another special young man, Matt. Matt was a friend and music partner of Michael's, like many of his associates. But what makes Matt stand tall in my spirit is his constant remembrance and respect for Michael, since time has passed on. Michael has been gone almost 14 years and yet Matt has regularly come to provide love and support to Ed and I, on more occasions than I can recall. Many of Michael's friends, although I know loved him dearly, have quite understandably moved on in their lives, moved away, gotten married and started their own families. Although they might reach out occasionally, Matt continues to come, regularly strengthening Ed and I. Matt has shown a tender and compassionate heart toward us. God bless him and his wife, and may the young family they are about to start share the love, comfort, care and compassion that Christ has extended to us through him, forever.

Last But Not Least

But many *who are* first will be last, and the last first. - Matthew 19:30

As I come to the end of this book, I feel to share one more earthly, unsolicited gift I received, to further illustrate the unlimited and unmerited favour of our merciful God.

Shortly after I started writing this book in the week leading up to Christmas 2020, I went to our neighbor jeweller, Rafael Jewellery, to replace the chain on the cross given to me some years ago by Jenny. I have been to this jeweller on a number of occasions and have come to understand Rafael is Christian, by his manner and his conversation.

On the day in question, I went in and he and his daughter were the only other people in the store. I explained why I needed a new chain again and asked if he could help in choosing one that would suit the cross and be a bit sturdier. I had a reckless habit, of being less than careful, in my attempts to take it off my neck, and thereby sometimes broke the links in the chain. He looked at my cross as he went to his cabinet and chose a suitable chain, which he handed to me. I assumed he handed it to me so I would look at it before purchasing it, but as I started to hand it back to him to pay for it, he simply said to me, "Merry Christmas."

I looked at him, first not understanding, then looked I at his daughter and back at him. They were both smiling at me, and I realized he was giving me the chain! I didn't know what to say - his generosity was so unexpected, so I simply thanked him and wished them both a Merry Christmas. I left with the newly gifted chain wondering how I could possibly repay him. As I neared writing the end of this book, it came to me: how better to repay his thoughtfulness than by commemorating his generosity in the closing chapter of this book. May God continue to bless him, his family and all those, like me, that he touches with his open kindness and his lovely reflection of Christ.

My spirit was lifted as I made my way home to share the news with my husband. I realized once more that I had been met with generosity, through God's spirit of giving, through the obedience of this jeweller to give me the chain. I accepted this precious gift from Rafael, but more significantly, from my Father, as an indication that He is well-pleased that I have undertaken this writing journey to share His love, His mercy, His grace and His loving-kindness, with you.

For my readers, I pray; **"The grace of the Lord Jesus Christ, and the love of God, and the communion of the Holy Spirit *be* with you all." - 2 Corinthians 13:14**

I thank You, Father, for all Your divine blessings, those seen and unseen. It has been my privilege to be called to write this book to honour You. Amen

ACKNOWLEDGEMENTS

I am the Alpha and the Omega, the Beginning and the End, the First and the Last. - Revelations 22:13

"First God, then you." – this is the sentiment shared with me, by Phyllis, years ago and it is ringing in my ears this morning as I sit to compose my acknowledgements. To my blessed Father God, first, I thank You Father for calling me and entrusting to me this task of love and praise. I thank You, for all You have shown me, for all You have given me, for life, for breath and most of all for my salvation through the death and resurrection of Your Son Jesus Christ. I thank You, Father, for my husband, and for my children and that You chose me to be their mother. I thank You that, through Sarah's comment the night Michael died - "Mommy we are so blessed, we had Michael for twenty-five years." - that I have been able to breathe and look at the blessing I had been given and not for what was taken away. I thank You, Father, for the infinite number of blessings, those seen and those unseen. I thank You, Father, for it is with great honour and privilege I submit this testimony of love to You.

Michael Henry George, my deceased son, *posthumously* for his laughter, his light, his loyalty and especially his love, generously imparted to me and everyone who knew him during his short time with us. I know he would be proud and overjoyed by this undertaking of love.

Georgiana Collington, my dear friend who generously wrote

the Foreword to this book. My confidante and spiritual advisor for inspired confirmation, encouragement and support since before this book began. Her companionship and dedication for reviewing each word written and offering spiritual insights that often opened my eyes to perspectives that I had not imagined. Just as the Father has given me so much, as illustrated by the wondrous stories in this book, He predestined that Georgiana was going to walk this path with me. I am forever grateful for her divine-inspired company all along this beautiful journey.

Edwardson George, my husband of 40 plus years, who let me, be me, in the writing of this book, despite the time it took away from us being together, in our newfound respective retirements. His devotion to Sarah and Chantal is unparalleled and Ed has walked by my side in the devastating loss of our son Michael. No parents should ever have to experience what we have shared in our loss of Michael, yet with the grace of Christ, and the blessings of Sarah, Chantal, and now Jon in our lives, together we stand strong, while Ed continues to hold my hand and my heart.

Sarah Mitchell, my youngest daughter was integral to my writing throughout this book, providing fresh eyes to some of my memories that were closer to my heart. Sarah, who has always provided clear perspectives on life that far transcend her years and gives me hope of things to come. I would like to thank her especially for the mom angel figurine she gave me inscribed with a beautiful sentiment of love, for her inspired paintings, and especially for my most treasured, and long sought-after, marching band.

Jonathon Mitchell, my son-in-law. I appreciate his prayers, encouragement and the "mom heart" he gave me reflecting the feeling in his heart toward me. I particularly appreciated his requests for updates of my writing progress all along the way, and his early "heads-up" that the writing would be the easy part.

Chantal Levesque, my oldest daughter, committed to her own family and life in Edmonton while always offering unconditional and unwavering love to our family. For the loving poem she composed to forever commemorate her love for her baby brother, "Blue." I will forever cherish these words in my heart, and lovingly display them in my prayer space. I thank her for her permission to share it with you in the pages of this book.

Karen Shepherd, my older sister, produced and gave me a picture photo book documenting Michael's life. She provided historical clarifications, encouragement, prophetic confirmations and prayers along this journey. Her insights and laughter all along the way strengthened me and inspired me to continue and to persevere, in all things, throughout our shared lives.

Lynn French, my baby sister, who provided encouragement, clarifications, support, laughter and prayers. I am grateful for her heartfelt letter which included a special impartation from God, and her permission to share it with you. Lynn has always been my loudest and proudest cheerleader throughout all my life, and even more so, since I began this writing journey.

Kevin Borden, my baby brother, who continually expresses the pride he feels that I have undertaken this writing journey and who has always been a lifelong, steadfast and loyal supporter of my personal and professional accomplishments.

Terry Ableson; of "Terry and Scherry," or "Scherry and Terry," recognized for her constant prayers, support and encouragement for all things in which we have partnered, laughed, cried and lived; always in-synch, together.

Malcolm Kelly, an author, former colleague, confidante, and valuable source of reference and advice to my early questions regarding publishing and editing.

Marie Baker, a dear friend and former colleague for generously providing her permission to use the copy of my picture, illustrated on the back cover.

Thank you to everyone whom I have written about, who have been, and in many cases continue to be, part of my life's journey. So many people, including so very many unnamed, have shared love, laughter, and tears as we shared this space and time as designed by our Father in heaven, I thank *each* of you.

This book began with my reading of Jonah around the beginning of November 2020, leading to writing at the beginning of December 2020, and directing me to begin this labour of love. It is not lost on me that, as I attended my time of devotion this morning, April 22, 2021 during my Bible reading, I turned the last page of Book of Revelation, reaching the end of the Bible, and today I have finished writing this book. *There are no coincidences in Christ.*

To God be all the glory.

Addendum:

I am preparing the final submission of my book after finishing the first draft on April 22, 2021. Much review and many revisions have since taken place and I am preparing to forward it to my publisher to begin the actual process to become a published author. I am pleased to report I have finished this on May 31, 2021 a few days before the June 3 deadline outlined to me in a dream back in December 2020.

You will notice a few occurrences that took place after May, including this statement, which I later inserted during the process of review.

To God, I give all the honour and praise for all good things.

EPILOGUE

That if you confess with your mouth the Lord Jesus and believe in your heart that God has raised Him from the dead, you will be saved. For with the heart one believes unto righteousness, and with the mouth confession is made unto salvation. - Romans 10:9-10

There is little left for me to share with you except to encourage you to open your hearts to hear the Lord. As you have read, He has favoured me immeasurably in my lifetime, and He can do the same for you and become an active participant in your life when you let Him in. I am living proof, of a living God!

If you haven't already accepted Jesus in your life, you can do that now, today, by believing in your heart and reciting out loud this Sinner's Prayer:

Sinner's Prayer

Blessed Father in heaven, I am a sinner. I believe Jesus Christ is Your Son and You sent Him to bear the pain and die on the cross for my sins. I repent of my sins. I believe that Jesus died and rose again; by His stripes I am healed and by His death and resurrection I am born again and called into Your kingdom. I declare Jesus Christ is Lord and invite Him into my heart and spirit and life today. I accept Jesus Christ as my Lord and Saviour. Thank You Father God for calling me and accepting me into Your kingdom. In the blessed name of Jesus, I pray. Amen

Hallelujah! If you've accepted Jesus by reciting and believing this prayer today, please reach out to a local church community for support and spiritual guidance in your walk with God.

May you be immeasurably blessed!

CPSIA information can be obtained
at www.ICGtesting.com
Printed in the USA
BVHW072133300122
627308BV00001B/5

9 781664 246959